Some of the Spheres of Holy Spirit Works

Book 2 of a trilogy about God the Holy Spirit

Michael E.J. Wright

malcolm down
PUBLISHING

Copyright © Michael E.J. Wright 2025

First published 2025 by Malcolm Down Publishing Ltd
www.malcolmdown.co.uk

28 27 26 25   7 6 5 4 3 2 1

The right of Michael E.J. Wright to be identified as the author of this work has been asserted by him in accordance with the Copyright, Designs and Patents Act 1988.

All rights reserved. No part of this publication may be reproduced, stored in a retrieval system, or transmitted in any other form or by any means, electronic, mechanical, photocopying, recording or otherwise, without the prior permission of the publisher.

British Library Cataloguing in Publication Data
A catalogue record for this book is available from the British Library.

ISBN: 978-1-917455-24-4

Unless otherwise indicated, Scripture quotations taken from the Holy Bible, New International Version (Anglicised edition). Copyright ©1979, 1984, 2011 by Biblica. Used by permission of Hodder & Stoughton Publishers, an Hachette UK company. All rights reserved.
'NIV' is a registered trademark of Biblica. UK trademark number 1448790.

Scripture quotations marked 'KJV' are from The Authorised (King James) Version. Rights in the Authorised Version in the United Kingdom are vested in the Crown. Reproduced by permission of the Crown's patentee, Cambridge University Press.

Scripture quotations from The New Testament in Modern English by J.B. Phillips copyright © 1960, 1972 J.B. Phillips. Administered by The Archbishops' Council of the Church of England. Used by Permission.

Scripture quotations marked 'NKJV' are taken from the Holy Bible, New King James Version®.
Copyright © 1982 by Thomas Nelson. Used by permission.
All rights reserved.

Cover design by Angela Selfe
Art direction by Sarah Grace

Printed in the UK

Content

Introduction: Greetings		5
1.	The Word	9
2.	New Birth and Baptism by the Spirit	23
3.	Baptism in the Holy Spirit	33
4.	Assurance	45
5.	Testimony	51
6.	Prayer and Worship	69
7.	Circumcision of the Heart by the Spirit	83
8.	Calls to Service and Ministry	107
9.	Leading and Guiding	123
10.	His Gifts	137
11.	His Fruit	159
12.	The Ministry Gifts	181
13.	Blasphemy, Grieving, Resisting or Pleasing the Holy Spirit	197
14.	Suffering	205
15.	The Blood	213
16.	The Centrality of Jesus	219
17.	The Exhortation of the Spirit in Harmony with Jesus to HEAR	229
Bibliography		231

Introduction

Greetings

Thank you for opening this book. Hopefully you will stay with it to the last page.

Initial comments

Through the writing period we have been progressively aware that the subject is enormous. Who are we to try to encompass with our feeble words the biblical teachings concerning God the Holy Spirit? We are neither theologians nor well-known expositors of Scripture, but we feel an urge to share with others what we have learnt, and in part experienced, of the blessed Paraclete.

You too probably long to know the Holy Spirit better; we pray that something in this book will spur you on in your pilgrimage. The Spirit himself will be your teacher, and it could well be that he will show you that, here and there, we have incorrectly or inadequately understood Scripture. Should this be the case, we suggest that you consult with others who evidently live in harmony with the Spirit and consistently manifest his fruit.

The gospel must be propagated; the world needs to hear that God is just, holy and love, that Jesus saves and that the church must be prepared for Jesus' return: accomplishment will come about, but only 'by the Spirit'.

Potential readers

The primary aspiration of the trilogy is to encourage Christian readers to accord more time and effort into reading and searching the scriptures, particularly, in our case, with regard to the person and work of the Holy Spirit.

This concerns all generations, folk who are in the whole range of spiritual experience, development and growth, i.e. the newly born-again, those who are keenly walking with and serving their Lord, those who are not so engaged, those who, for a variety of reasons, have many demands on their time and energy (including further education, apprenticeships, intensive professional commitments, family life, caring for elderly, disabled and suffering family members and others and so on), and also those who feel called to ministries which would benefit from full- or part-time attendance at a Bible college.

We also have in mind local church leaders who work full-time in their trade or profession, for whom we aspire to furnish useful material for ministry concerning God the Holy Spirit.

Teaching

The trilogy is centred on the theme of teaching, and since successful teaching involves much repetition, we ask our readers to tolerate the repetition they will find, including in the remaining books of the trilogy.

Bible versions

Except where otherwise indicated we have chosen to use and quote from the New International Version (NIV) of the Bible, 2011 anglicised version. Where other versions are used the following abbreviations indicate their identity:

- KJV for the King James Version.
- NKJV for the New King James Version.
- NIV 1984 for older version of the NIV.

In some places you will see parts of the quote in bold; this is our emphasis.

References

The words to the hymns I referred to can be found at https://hymnary.org, unless an alternative source is specified in the text.

Acknowledgements

Firstly, I wish to mention the patience and support of my wife Lucie D. Grimaldi. Other members of our family have helped, some from the start, others, particularly our granddaughter Clara, in the preparation of the book for publication.

Michael Wright

1
The Word

'Words' is a topic that crops up frequently on *Pointless*, a popular and often amusing quiz show on television. Some of the participants are very good at 'words', others struggle! Dear reader, how are you on the words in the ancient Hebrew and Greek texts of the Old and New Testaments translated 'word' or 'words' in English? One which you probably know is *logos* (Greek), but there are others, and it is helpful to take note of some of them prior to moving on in our subject, 'The Holy Spirit and the Word'. Here are the 'words' that appear to be the most essential to our present purpose; all of them are everything but pointless, and, hopefully, they and their several applications will stimulate our thinking and praying:

Hebrew (OT): *dabar* and its synonym *imrah,* e.g. Psalm 119:11, 'I have hidden your **word** in my heart that I might not sin against you', the root meaning being 'to speak or talk'. We have a Creator who speaks to us, and he talks with us. Psalm 119 is a major treatise on *dabar.*

Greek (NT): *rhema,* root meaning 'that which is spoken, or what is uttered in speech or writing'. Typical phrases in English are 'The **word** of the Lord' and 'The **word** of God', e.g. Luke 3:2, 'The **word** of God came to John [the Baptist] ... in the wilderness.' A short while later Jesus said to the tempter 'Man shall not live on bread alone, but on every [*rhema*] that comes from the mouth of God' (Matthew 4:4).

Logos, which carries the meaning 'expression of thought' and is found in such New Testament phrases as 'word of truth', 'word of God', 'word of Jesus', 'word of Christ' and 'keep the word', e.g. Colossians 3:16, 'Let the **word** of Christ dwell in you richly as you teach' (NIV 1984). However, the pre-eminent use of *logos,* by far, is as the Personal Word. In John's writings Jesus, the Christ, the Son of God, God the Son, **is the Word (*the Logos*)**. 'In the beginning was **the Word**, and **the Word** was with God, and **the Word** was God' (John 1:1). '**The Word** became flesh and made his dwelling among us' (v.14). These are majestic statements, and they enshrine the wonderful truth of the incarnation of God the Son as the Son of Man. The God-Man Jesus is the Word, the expression of the Father! For further thoughts on this please see my comments on the role of the Holy Spirit in the incarnation of the Son of God in Book 3. At a later date John, writing to believers in general, testified thus: 'That which was from the beginning ... which ... our hands have touched – this we proclaim concerning **the Word** of life' (1 John 1:1).

Didache, root meaning 'teaching' and often used to embody the whole of Jesus' and the early church's teaching and doctrine; so we encounter the phrases 'the teaching', 'my teaching' and 'his teaching', e.g. Mark 1:22, 'The people were amazed at **his teaching**.' *Didache* is most generally used regarding oral or written teaching using language, but it can also be used of teaching by demonstration or example.

It is twice translated '**word** of instruction' in 1 Corinthians, that is in 14:6 and 14:26, and in this form *didache* is one of contributions that a Christian can bring to an assembly of believers.

Martyreo, translated 'spread the **word**' in John 12:17, and that is what the crowd did after witnessing Lazarus coming out alive from the tomb in which he had been buried, and it is what Christians have been doing since the day of Pentecost, often at great personal cost; we note the close link of *martyreo* to martyr.

The role of the Holy Spirit

The Spirit's role in the incarnation of the Son of God has been noted; it cannot be overemphasised. From conception Jesus was the Word, the ***Logos***, and this he continued to be after his birth; he was, and is, the expression to mankind of the mind and heart of the Father. He was always indwelt by the fullness of the Spirit, and furthermore the anointing of the Spirit with power came upon him immediately after he was baptised by John, and the Spirit remained on him. He became the anointed Word who, by oral teaching, by demonstration, by illustration, by attitude, by example and by all the other means of expression he used, transmitted knowledge, wisdom, instruction and gospel to us all.

After Jesus' ascension, and the outpouring of the Holy Spirit at Pentecost, it became the task of Christians to communicate the word, the knowledge of Jesus (the Personal Word) and the gospel in all its fullness, throughout the world. The mission is difficult, challenging, costly and glorious, and it can only be accomplished by the help and enablement of the Spirit. The Word we are called to share, to disseminate, is the Living Word, because it is infused in all its forms by the person and dynamic of the Holy Spirit.

The New Testament associates **the word spoken** by the early Christians with the person and action of the Holy Spirit:

Shortly after Pentecost and the subsequent healing of a crippled beggar, Peter and John were brought before the Sanhedrin. 'Peter, **filled with the Holy Spirit, said** ... "it is by the name of Jesus Christ of Nazareth, whom you crucified but whom God raised from the dead, that this man stands before you healed"' (Acts 4:8-10).

Released by the Sanhedrin, Peter and John, together with other Christians, prayed using words from Psalm 2, 'Sovereign Lord you made the heavens and the earth and the sea, and everything in them. **You spoke by the Holy Spirit through** the mouth of your servant, our father **David**: "Why do the nations rage? . . . the rulers band together against the Lord and against his anointed one"' (Acts 4:24-26). Verse 31 affirms, 'After they prayed, the place where they were meeting was shaken. And they were **all filled with the Holy Spirit** and **spoke the word of God boldly**.'

Other passages in Acts tell how the Holy Spirit endued the spoken word concerning Jesus and the gospel with power and authority, e.g. the ministry of Peter in Cornelius' house (10:44-48 and 11:15-17); Paul's final statement to the leaders of the Jews at Rome, 'The Holy Spirit spoke the truth to your ancestors' (Acts 28:25).

The Letters are not silent on the matter; 2 Peter 1:20-21 exhorts, 'Above all, you must understand that no prophecy of Scripture came about by the prophet's own interpretation of things. For prophecy never had its origin in human will, but **prophets, though human, spoke from God** as they were carried along **by the Holy Spirit.**' The phrase 'carried along' sets our imaginations into high motion! Let us pray that Christians reading God's word today, testifying, teaching or preaching from it, will be similarly 'carried along' by the Spirit.

We should also note that right at the beginning of time, space and the creation of matter, the Son of God (the Word) and the Holy Spirit (the Breath or *ruâh*) acted in divine harmony to create from nothing, and to sustain thereafter, all things that are:

The Son [the Word] is the image of the invisible God, the firstborn over all creation. For in him all things were created: things in heaven and on earth, visible and invisible, whether thrones or powers or rulers or authorities; all things were created through him and for him. He is before all things, and in him all things hold together. (Colossians 1:15-17)

*He [God] has **spoken** to us by his Son, whom he appointed heir of all things, and through whom also he made the universe . . . sustaining all things by his **powerful word**. (Hebrews 1:2-3)*

*In the beginning God created the heavens and the earth . . . and the **Spirit of God** was hovering over the waters. (Genesis 1:1-2)*

*The LORD God formed a man from the dust of the ground and breathed into his nostrils the **breath [the ruâh] of life**. (Genesis 2:7)*

These and other passages of Scripture combine to teach us that the awesome creative power of the word spoken by he who 'in the beginning was the Word' brought all that is into being, over which the omnipotent and omniscient Spirit hovered, imparting life and vigour to that which till then was inanimate.

The intimate and harmonious combined working of the Personal Word, Jesus Christ, and the Holy Spirit is clearly set forth in Scripture, and we are deeply aware of our need to be more and more conscious of this in our everyday living, and in the propagation of the gospel. It must therefore be God's will that the words that Jesus' disciples speak be inspired, endued with grace, wisdom, truth, love and authority by the enabling and empowering Holy Spirit. Logically this should apply in ordinary conversation, in verbal testimony concerning Jesus and the gospel, in what we say in our working or professional roles, in teaching and preaching, in short in all that we say! Is anyone up to this? Probably not! And that is where the challenge lies; at my door and yours.

There are times and places in the lives of all Christians when and where there is a particular and pressing need for inspired speech, that is the use of words given by the Holy Spirit. In the context of the teaching he was giving to his disciples concerning the end times Jesus said, 'Whenever you are arrested and brought to trial, do not worry beforehand about what to say. Just say whatever is given you at the time, for it is not you speaking, but the Holy Spirit' (Mark 13:11). At this point, please pause a while in order to pray for fellow believers, worldwide, who need to put this counsel into practice.

This brings us to the recorded word, **the written word**. Written on papyrus or paper or transmitted over the ether onto our screens ... all very important, but more important than these are the writing tablets highlighted by Paul in his second letter to the Corinthian Christians.

> *You show that you are a letter from Christ, the result of our ministry, **written** not with ink but **with the Spirit of the living God**, not on tablets of stone but on tablets of human hearts ... He [God] has made us competent as ministers of a new covenant – not of the letter but of the Spirit; for the letter kills, but the Spirit gives life. (2 Corinthians 3:3,6)*

This remarkable statement tells of the word written by the Spirit on receptive hearts, and it prompts us to ask what has the Spirit written on my heart, your heart, today? The obvious associated thought is, 'Maybe there is need to ask the Spirit to erase unholy writings that are taking up space in our hearts and minds.'

The word written by the Spirit, generally in ink, or similar

One day Jesus wrote in the sand. Only a handful of persons had the privilege of reading what he wrote, and the effect on them was dramatic (John 8:6-8).

About one and a half millennia earlier God wrote the ten commandments on two stone tablets:

> *Moses turned and went down the mountain with the two tablets of the covenant law in his hands. They were inscribed on both sides, front and back. The tablets*

were the work of God; the writing was the writing of God, engraved on the tablets. (Exodus 32:15-16)

The impact of this 'writing of God' upon Israel and the whole of mankind is impossible to encompass.

On another occasion the finger of God wrote on a wall a message of judgment addressed to a proud and idolatrous king (see Daniel 5).

Each of these divine communications was expressed in a language known by, or interpretable for, the recipients. This is a characteristic of all forms of the written word of God.

Writings inspired by the Holy Spirit, put onto suitable supports by persons appointed by God, expressed in languages and terms understood and clear to earthlings, and included, initially (the Old Testament) by the leaders of the Jewish people and then by leaders of the church militant (the Old and New Testament) in the collection of documents we know as the Bible, are the Christian Scriptures.

The often-quoted verses 16-17 in chapter 3 of Paul's second letter to Timothy are very important in this connection. They read:

All Scripture is God-breathed [the work of the Spirit] and is useful for teaching, rebuking, correcting and training in righteousness, so that the servant of God may be thoroughly equipped for every good work.

We wholeheartedly believe these verses but, from time to time, when reading and studying the Bible many of us find that we are occasionally in difficulty regarding some books or passages. Happily, God the Holy Spirit comes to our aid, and he either clarifies our minds or advises us to leave the issue in his hands. It is, of course, important to have an understanding regarding what we are meant to understand by 'all Scripture'.

The writings that would be considered 'Scripture' were recognised by God's people as inspired very early on. The Old Testament was already accepted by the time of Jesus' birth and the core of the New Testament was agreed upon by the middle of the 2nd century, even if it took another couple of centuries before the full list was made official.

The Spirit who had inspired the writers also guided our forefathers to a happy and united conclusion. Since those early centuries relatively minor differences of opinion and conviction have surfaced, but today's Christians have the witness of the Spirit that the Bible they read, that nourishes their communion with the Lord and with each other, is Scripture, the written Word of God.

Paul draws Timothy's attention to some of the many purposes (teaching, etc.) to which Scripture should be put. In so doing Christians need to be guided and inspired by the same Spirit who breathed upon the writers.

Parallel to the passage in 2 Timothy we should mention again:

> *Above all, you must understand that no prophecy of Scripture came about by the prophet's own interpretation of things. For prophecy never had its origin in the human will, but prophets, though human, spoke from God as they were carried along by the Holy Spirit. (2 Peter 1:20-21)*

These verses attest to the origin of Scripture and by extension tell us how Scripture becomes a living dynamic in our lives; when we step into the slip stream of the Spirit, we too are carried along by him and the written word becomes the living word in us.

John's gospel chapter 3 records Jesus' teaching on the New Birth, which, he said, comes about by the combined action of the Word (symbolised by water) and the Holy Spirit. This Word, energised by the Spirit, is 'the Word of truth' by which 'he chose to give us birth' (James 1:18, see also Titus 3:5).

Romans 8:16: 'The Spirit himself testifies with our spirit that we are God's children.' The Holy Spirit often testifies to our spirit directly, or by using a vast variety of things and factors, but Christians commonly experience divine testimony via the written Word.

Hebrews 4:12: 'For the word of God is alive and active. Sharper than any double-edged sword, it penetrates even to dividing soul and spirit, joints and marrow; it judges the thoughts and attitudes of the heart.' The convicting and incisive nature of God's Word (*a priori* the written Word) is very similar to the Holy Spirit's work, as taught by Jesus: 'He will prove the world to be in the wrong about sin and righteousness and judgment' (John 16:8). Although, it would seem, written primarily for persons not yet Christian, these verses have figured large in the experience of believers in times of spiritual awakening. Clearly the written Word and the Spirit work in tandem. In this connection, please see chapter 7 'Circumcision of the Heart by the Spirit'.

When Jesus explained his Parable of the Sower to his disciples he said, 'The seed is the word of God' (Luke 8:11). Jesus did not say so, but you may agree that it is edifying to think of the rainfall that follows the sowing, and the sun's warming rays, as symbolic of the Holy Spirit and his work.

Metaphors in Scripture for the Word of God

The metaphors for the Word of God that we find in the Bible are strongly reminiscent of those used to speak of the Holy Spirit. An eloquent example is Jeremiah 23:29: '"Is not my Word like fire," declares the LORD, "and like a hammer that breaks a rock in pieces?"' Believers who have known God's burning and breaking work in their lives readily acknowledge that it has been the combined working of the written Word and the Holy Spirit that has been dealing with them in grace.

This is borne out by Harold Morton in *Messages That Made the [Methodist] Revival*. He writes:

> *A little company of earnest men immersed themselves for years in the study of the Bible . . . as a whole. So intent were they on the things of God that they could not get away from his Word. It drew them as the moth is drawn to the flame. 'Bible Moths', men called them in derision; but these moths were not burned up, they were only kindled by the flame. They burned with fire and yet were not consumed. They made their dwelling place the wondrous Word in which the breath of God is ever moving and the Spirit of Fire entered into them, purified them, set their souls on fire.*[1]

---

1. Harold Morton, *Messages That Made the Revival* (London, Epworth 1 Press, 1920), p.16.

Many then and since have followed John Wesley's example; his purpose was to be a 'man of one book' (*Homo unius libri*).[2]

Ephesians 6:17 tells us that the Word of God is a sword; as such the Word is an essential part of a Christian's weaponry and armoury. Furthermore, the word of God is 'the sword of the Spirit' and consequently invincible in defence and conquest. The 'sword' wielded by the Spirit is mighty in the advance of the Kingdom and in the defence of God's honour and of his people. Dear reader, do you have recollections of God's sword piercing your conscience and your heart, bringing you to an awareness of your need of Jesus the Saviour? Are we all convinced that fruitful evangelism, spiritual awakenings and revivals can only come about because of the Holy Spirit using the Word to bring people to conviction of sin, of God's holiness and of judgment?

Extracts from four hymns

By William Cowper:

> *The Spirit breathes upon the Word,*
> *And brings the truth to sight;*
> *Precepts and promises afford,*
> *A sanctifying light.*[3]

By Charles Wesley:

> *While now Thine oracles we read*
> *With earnest prayer and strong desire,*

---

2. *Wesley's Standard Sermons, Volume I*, p.264.
3. William Cowper (1779), 'The Spirit Breathes Upon the Word', https://hymnary.org/text/the_spirit_breathes_upon_the_word (accessed 23.3.24)

> *O let Thy Spirit from Thee proceed,*
> *Our souls to awaken and inspire,*
> *Our weakness help, our darkness chase,*
> *And guide us by the light of grace.*[4]

Also, by Charles Wesley:

> *Whate'er the ancient prophets spoke*
> *Concerning Thee, O Christ, make known,*
> *Sole subject of the sacred Book,*
> *Thou fillest all, and Thou alone;*
> *Yet there our Lord we cannot see,*
> *Unless Thy Spirit lend the key.'*[5]

And finally, Charles Wesley again:

> *Come now, everlasting Spirit,*
> *Bring to every thankful mind*
> *All the Saviour's dying merit,*
> *Sufferings for all humankind;*
>
> *True Recorder of his passion,*
> *Now the living faith impart,*
> *Now reveal his great salvation,*
> *Preach his gospel to our heart.*[6]

---

4. Charles Wesley (1707–1788), 'Inspirer of the Ancient Seers', https://hymnary.org/text/inspirer_of_the_ancient_seers (accessed 23.3.24).
5. Charles Wesley (1707–1788), 'Come Then, Thou Prophet of the Lord', https://hymnary.org/text/come_then_thou_prophet_of_the_lord (accessed 23.3.24).
6. Charles Wesley (1745), 'Come, Thou Everlasting Spirit', https://hymnary.org/text/come_thou_everlasting_spirit (accessed 23.3.24).

2
New Birth and Baptism by the Spirit

These lines are being written at Christmas time, a season when one of the greatest pleasures for English-speaking Christians is to participate in the singing of Charles Wesley's wonderful hymn 'Hark! The Herald Angels Sing'. This carol is a delightful statement of several cardinal features of the Christian faith; its third verse reads:

> *Hail the heaven born Prince of Peace!*
> *Hail the Sun of Righteousness!*
> *Light and life to all he brings,*
> *Risen with healing in his wings.*
> *Mild he lays his glory by,*
> *Born that we no more may die,*
> *Born to raise us from the earth,*
> ***Born to give us second birth.*** [7]

---

7. Charles Wesley (1739), 'Hark! The Herald Angels Sing', https://hymnary.org/text/hark_the_herald_angels_sing_glory_to (accessed 24.3.24).

Sung to the accompaniment of Mendelssohn's uplifting and gladsome music, the phrase 'born to give us second birth' affords believers an opportunity to engage in intense worship of the Saviour who has brought us to new birth.

The term 'new birth' occurs once in the Bible: 'In his great mercy he [God the Father] has given us **new birth** into a living hope through the resurrection of Jesus Christ from the dead' (1 Peter 1:3). For parents the birth of their children gives them hope for the future, and Peter reminds us that the new birth places the child of God into a relationship of living hope with the Father. And Hebrews 6:19 affirms that, due to this new relationship, 'We have this hope as an anchor for the soul, firm and secure.'

With the exception of Nicodemus' incredulous remark (see text cited below), the term 'second birth' does not occur in the Bible, but 'born again' does; the word 'again' implies that at least two births are in view (there are of course not more than two), and this justifies Wesley's term 'second birth'. The record in John 3 of Jesus' conversation with Israel's teacher, Nicodemus, is certainly the key passage concerning being born again. Here are verses 1-10, but readers would find it helpful to continue to verse 21.

> *Now there was a Pharisee, a man named Nicodemus who was a member of the Jewish ruling council. He came to Jesus at night and said, 'Rabbi, we know that you are a teacher who has come from God. For no one could perform the signs you are doing if God were not with him.' Jesus replied, 'Very truly I tell you, no one can see the kingdom of God unless they are born again.' 'How can someone be born when they are old?' Nicodemus asked. 'Surely they cannot enter*

a second time into their mother's womb to be born!' Jesus answered, 'Very truly I tell you, no one can enter the kingdom of God unless they are born of water and the Spirit. Flesh gives birth to flesh, but the Spirit gives birth to spirit. You should not be surprised at my saying, "You must be born again." The wind blows wherever it pleases. You hear its sound, but you cannot tell where it comes from or where it is going. So it is with everyone born of the Spirit.' 'How can this be?' Nicodemus asked. 'You are Israel's teacher,' said Jesus, 'and do you not understand these things?'

Why did Jesus consider that Nicodemus ought to have understood what he said to him about 'being born again'? John Wesley was of the view that the term was in common use when Nicodemus was Israel's teacher. It was used when an adult Gentile, 'convinced that the Jewish religion was of God . . . desired to join therein . . . was baptised . . . and was said to be born again'.[8] Nevertheless, Nicodemus, well versed as he no doubt was in scripture and Jewish custom, was perplexed by the Master's words. It seems that he did not understand that natural birth, even into a Jewish family, does not afford right of entry into God's kingdom, nor does it do more than convey to every child born of man and woman the fallen, sinful nature of Adam and Eve. Death and non-admittance into the Kingdom is the judgment and condemnation that God has passed on all; this, Jesus taught, is the way of all flesh. But, wonder of wonders, there is a way out of this dreadful and hopeless situation; it is, Jesus said, to be born again, not naturally, not of the flesh, but of water and of the Spirit. In the

---

8. *Wesley's Standard Sermons, Volume II*, Sermon XXXIX, The New Birth, p.232.

prologue to his gospel John wrote, 'To all who did receive him, to those who believed in his name, he gave the right to become children of God – children born not of natural descent, nor of human decision or a husband's will, but born of God' (John 1:12-13).

By combining the teaching in chapters 1 and 3 of John's gospel we see that 'receiving' Jesus is the same as being 'born again'; it is being 'born of God', or 'born of water and the Spirit', and it affords entry into God's family and his kingdom. Now, prior to moving on further we must acknowledge that for most of us the John 3 dialogue begs a question centred on the word 'water'. What is the water by which we must be born again? Many Christians and not a few denominations, maintain that Jesus was speaking of baptism, water baptism, and they teach that by baptism a person is born again and, by means of the sacrament, enters the kingdom of God. This is not our position. We do believe that Christians should be baptised in water as soon as possible after their conversion, i.e. after coming to Jesus as repentant sinners, to receive him into their lives as Saviour and Lord. Water baptism is thus understood to be a public reaffirmation of a personal and very real experience, which has already taken place, of the saving grace of Jesus Christ, together with identification with him in his death, burial and resurrection (see Romans 6:3-14). There are many examples in Acts which demonstrate that in early church times persons baptised in water were already Christians, born again and in a family relationship with Jesus Christ and the Father.

What then should we understand the water necessary for new birth to be? Our conviction is that it is the 'water' of the Word of God, i.e. the Spoken and Written Word of God.

To substantiate this please consider the following:

1 Peter 1:23-25: 'You have been born again, not of perishable seed, but of imperishable, **through the living and enduring word of God**... the word of the Lord endures for ever.'

James 1:18: 'He [the Father] chose to give us birth **through the word of truth**, that we might be a kind of firstfruits of all he created.'

Ephesians 5:25-26: 'Christ loved the church and gave himself up for her to make her holy, cleansing her by **the washing with water through the word.**'

This passage speaks of the initial washing (the new birth), and the continual washing thereafter, through the word, until the day when Christ will present the church to himself as a radiant and perfect bride.

The Holy Spirit uses the word of God to convict, convince, cleanse and re-create the repentant. The Spirit and the word combine, in full cooperation with the all-powerful blood of the Lord Jesus Christ, to effect new birth. The Greek word *anagennao* has two parts: *ana*, 'again, or from above', and *gennao,* 'to beget'. Consequently, a born-again person has been begotten of God (not of man), from above (not earthly, not of time and space) and is immortal.

2 Corinthians 5:17: 'If anyone is in Christ, the new creation has come: the old has gone, the new is here!'

Galatians 6:15: 'Neither circumcision nor uncircumcision means anything; what counts is the new creation.'

The new birth implies that all things have become new, with a new beginning, a new family (Ephesians 2:19), a new nature

(2 Peter 1:4), a new lifestyle and character (Ephesians 4:20-24), a new name (Revelation 3:12), a new song (Revelation 5:9), a new destiny with participation and presence in the new Jerusalem, the new heaven and the new earth (Revelation 21:1-2), a new commandment to obey (John 13:34) and a new mission to accomplish (Matthew 28:19-20).

Each of these new things is very wonderful and worthy of extensive and close appreciation, but we comment further on only the **new nature** which Christians have by virtue of the new birth. The passage in 2 Peter 1:3-4 says that God's 'divine power has given us [the born again] everything we need for a godly life through our knowledge of him who called us by his own glory and goodness. Through these he has given us his very great and precious promises, so that through them you may **participate in the divine nature**, having escaped the corruption in the world caused by evil desires'.

We, and we presume many of our readers too, are very much aware of having two natures: the first we received as a part of our natural conception and birth; the second was implanted in us when we were born again, i.e. when Jesus became our personal Saviour and Lord. The two natures are in conflict. Reading Romans chapter 7 gives graphic proof that the apostle Paul was deeply aware of the battle of the two natures being waged within him. Happily, he was also totally convinced that in Christ victory for the new nature is assured. With him we say, 'Thanks be to God – through Jesus Christ our Lord (*we are overcomers*)!' We can also be assured that the two who gave us new birth, the Word and the Spirit, are our source of strength in the day-after-day conflict of our natures.

A legendary long-lived Egyptian bird associated with the sun, and known as a phoenix, had, according to some, a life cycle of 500 years; at the end of each cycle the bird was consumed by fire, and from the ashes another phoenix arose. But the creature had the same nature as previously; it was the same old phoenix! The wonder of the new birth is that it implies a new nature, the nature of Christ implanted in a human being:

Colossians 1:27 tells of 'the glorious riches of this mystery, which is Christ in you, the hope of glory'.

> Those who are in the realm of the flesh cannot please God. You, however, are not in the realm of the flesh but are in the realm of the Spirit, if indeed the Spirit of God lives in you. And if anyone does not have the Spirit of Christ, they do not belong to Christ. But if Christ is in you, then even though your body is subject to death because of sin, the Spirit gives life because of righteousness. And if the Spirit of him who raised Jesus from the dead is living in you, he who raised Christ from the dead will also give life to your mortal bodies because of his Spirit who lives in you. (Romans 8:8-11)

Simply put, because Jesus, the Christ, and the Holy Spirit live in the believer, he has a new nature with which he will live for evermore. This is new birth, new life, abundant life, eternal life by the Spirit and by the word.

Ephesians 4:22-24 exhorts us to put off our old nature (self), which is constantly 'being corrupted by its deceitful desires', so that we might be 'made new in the attitude of [our] minds; and to put on the new self [nature], created to be like God in true righteousness and holiness'. Here we realise that in order to progress in God after conversion, the new birth, we must wholeheartedly cooperate with the Spirit and the word. Thereby our sisters and brethren in Christ, and the folk amongst whom we live, will realise that we are indeed 'a new creation'.

Baptism *by* the Spirit

None can fully describe, fully explain or understand the many extraordinary things that happen when a person is born again. Perhaps the most amazing of these new things is described, with simple words, in 1 Corinthians 12:13: 'We were all baptised by one Spirit so as to form one body —whether Jews or Gentiles, slave or free – and we were all given the one Spirit to drink.' We understand this to mean that, at new birth, the newborn is instantly placed into (plunged into) the body of Christ, the church. At this point each and every believer enters God's family, the community of the firstborn, the universal priesthood with all the adherent privileges and responsibilities. This is awesome and overwhelming, and we must take comfort and re-assurance from the fact that we begin as little children and will be cared for in consequence by our heavenly Father, our great Elder Brother and by our older sisters and brothers in the Family. Furthermore, the Holy Spirit and the word who brought us to new birth will be our strength, our guide and our vision as we grow in grace.

A thought from C.S. Lewis:

> *The more we let God take over, the more truly ourselves we become, because he made us. He invented all the different people you and I were intended to be . . .*

> it is when I turn to Christ, when I give myself to his personality, that I begin to have a real personality of my own.[9]

Another, from John Wesley, concerning the mystery of how the Holy Spirit accomplishes the 'born again' work:

> We are not to expect any minute, philosophical account of the manner how this is done. Our Lord sufficiently guards us against any such expectation, by the words immediately following the text ('Ye must be born again'), wherein he reminds Nicodemus of as indisputable a fact as any in the whole compass of nature, which, notwithstanding, the wisest man under the sun is not able fully to explain. 'The wind bloweth where it listeth,'—not by any power or wisdom; 'and thou hearest the sound thereof,'—thou art absolutely assured, beyond all doubt, that it doth blow; 'but thou canst not tell whence it cometh, nor whither it goeth,'—the precise manner how it begins and ends, rises and falls, no man can tell. 'So is every one that is born of the Spirit': thou mayest be as absolutely assured of the fact, as of the blowing of the wind; but the precise manner how it is done, how the Holy Spirit works this in the soul, neither thou, nor the wisest of the children of men, is able to explain.[10]

---

9. C.S. Lewis, *Mere Christianity* (New York: Touchstone, a division of Simon & Schuster, 1996), p.190.
10. *Wesley's Standard Sermons, Volume II*, Sermon XXXIX, The New Birth, p.231. (Bible citations from John 3, KJV.)

3

Baptism in the Holy Spirit

This is an extremely important subject, and on it Christians have different and diverse positions. How to understand biblical teaching on the matter, and how to appreciate the testimonies of folk who tell of what the experience means to them, are questions to which millions of Christians have sought answers. In the main (but there are no doubt many variations) it would seem that there are broadly two approaches, the first being those who believe that baptism in the Holy Spirit is part and parcel of being born again, i.e. integral to conversion. Here we would comment that there is a baptism which is a very wonderful aspect of the new birth, and it is clearly set forth in 1 Corinthian 12:13, 'For by one Spirit are we all baptized into one body' (KJV). This verse says that the Holy Spirit places (plunges) the believer into Christ's body, the church. The active role of baptising is fulfilled by the Holy Spirit, and the passive role is that of the church (the body of Christ), who receives and welcomes the newborn child of God into the fold. (Please see chapter 2 in this book on 'New Birth and Baptism by the Spirit' for further comment.)

Others, and we identify with these, believe that baptism in the Holy Spirit is separate from, and usually subsequent to, the new birth. In essence this baptism is an endowment of power to the believer in order to facilitate and authenticate witness to the person and work of Jesus. 'You will receive power when the Holy Spirit comes on you; and you will be my witnesses in Jerusalem, and in all Judea and Samaria, and to the ends of the earth' (Acts 1:8).

Let us now take note of several passages of scripture; they are self-explanatory and do not need lengthy exposition in order to be understood.

John the Baptist compares his ministry with that of Jesus:

> *I baptise you with water for repentance. But after me comes one who is more powerful than I, whose sandals I am not worthy to carry.* **He will baptise you with the Holy Spirit and fire.** *(Matthew 3:11)*

Further testimony from John the Baptist; he explains that God had told him that 'the man on whom you see the Spirit come down and remain is **the one who will baptise with the Holy Spirit**' (John 1:33).

Very shortly before his ascension Jesus says to his apostles, 'Do not leave Jerusalem, but wait for the gift my Father promised, which you have heard me speak about. For John baptised with water, but in a few days you will be baptised with the Holy Spirit' (Acts 1:4-5). For the 'promise of the Father' see John 14:16-26.

The first accomplishment of the promise is related in Acts 2:1-4:

> When the day of Pentecost came, they were all together in one place. Suddenly a sound like the blowing of a violent wind came from heaven and filled the whole house where they were sitting. They saw what seemed to be tongues of fire that separated and came to rest on each of them. **All of them were filled with the Holy Spirit** and began to speak in other tongues as the Spirit enabled them.

Peter explains to the cosmopolitan crowd assembled in Jerusalem for participation in the Feast of Pentecost, 'Exalted to the right hand of God, he [Jesus] has received from the Father the promised Holy Spirit and has poured out what you now see and hear' (Acts 2:33). Sometime later a newly evangelised and converted group in Samaria similarly received the Holy Spirit.

> When they [Peter and John] arrived, they prayed for the new believers there that they might receive the Holy Spirit, because the Holy Spirit had not yet come on any of them; they had simply been baptised in the name of the Lord Jesus. Then Peter and John placed their hands on them, and **they received the Holy Spirit** (Acts 8:15-17)

The next chapter of Acts records the conversion of Saul of Tarsus. He was en route for Damascus with the evil intent of doing great harm to 'the Lord's disciples' living in that city, when, nearing the town, he had an awesome encounter with the risen Christ. The man was humbled, broken and temporarily blinded, and he confessed Jesus as his Lord! He entered Damascus and lodged there. Three days later, in a vision, the Lord charged a disciple with a mission which, at first, he found very unpalatable, and he said so to the Lord! Acts 9:15-19 tells what happened next:

> *The Lord said to Ananias, 'Go! This man is my chosen instrument to proclaim my name to the Gentiles and their kings and to the people of Israel. I will show him how much he must suffer for my name.' Then Ananias went to the house and entered it. Placing his hands on Saul, he said, 'Brother Saul, the Lord – Jesus, who appeared to you on the road as you were coming here – has sent me so that you may see again and* **be filled with the Holy Spirit**.*' Immediately, something like scales fell from Saul's eyes, and he could see again. He got up and was baptised, and after taking some food, he regained his strength.*

We note that in Saul's experience the sequence was conversion, followed by baptism (filling) with the Holy Spirit, followed by baptism in water. From this time on the power of the Spirit was clearly on display in Saul/Paul's life and ministry.

Moving on to the tenth chapter of Acts we find the inspiring account of the conversion, Spirit receiving and water baptism of a large group of persons comprising the relatives and close friends of a man named Cornelius, a centurion in the Roman army. Cornelius, a God-fearing man, heeding the instructions he had received from an angel in a vision, had invited Peter to come to his house in order to speak of everything the Lord had commanded him to tell. Peter began by saying that he had now come to realise that God does not show favouritism but accepts people from every nation who fear him and do what is right. He spoke of Jesus of Nazareth, his works, death, resurrection and post-resurrection appearances, and he concluded with, 'All the prophets testify about him that everyone who believes in him receives forgiveness of sins through his name' (Acts 10:43).

Then, says the record:

> *While Peter was still speaking these words,* **the Holy Spirit came on all who heard the message.** *The circumcised believers who had come with Peter were astonished that the gift of the Holy Spirit had been poured out even on Gentiles. For they heard them speaking in tongues and praising God. Then Peter said, 'Surely no one can stand in the way of their being baptised with water. They have received the Holy Spirit just as we have.' So he ordered that they be baptised in the name of Jesus Christ. Then they asked Peter to stay with them for a few days. (v.44-48)*

Those few days must have been very special for all concerned! This group of newly born again, Holy Spirit filled and water baptised Gentiles had received power to be witnesses to Jesus, and no doubt that is what they became.

Thus far we have given attention to a group of Jewish disciples (perhaps numbering 120) at Jerusalem, a company probably of mixed race in Samaria, an individual named Saul/Paul, a learned Jew, and a Gentile company of family and friends. We will now look at the report in Acts 19 concerning a group of about twelve men at Ephesus. Maybe they were a mixed group of Jews and non-Jews; women also may have been present but the text is silent on the matter. The men had become Christians under the ministry of Apollos, a travelling teacher who preached Christ but was deficient in knowledge concerning water baptism and the person of the Holy Spirit. The converts were the image of their mentor; they knew Jesus as their Lord and Saviour, had received water baptism but only as it was taught by John the Baptist (i.e. a baptism of repentance but not a baptism of identification with Jesus in his death, burial and resurrection), and they had not received the baptism with the Holy Spirit. The new birth they had received had of course been accomplished by the Holy Spirit, but they lacked the subsequent filling of the Spirit. To Paul they said, 'We have not even heard that there is a Holy Spirit' (Acts 19:2).

What happened after this is related in verses 4-6:

> *Paul said, 'John's baptism was a baptism of repentance. He told the people to believe in the one coming after him, that is in Jesus.' On hearing this, they were baptised in the name of the Lord Jesus. When Paul placed his hands on them,* **the Holy Spirit came on them***, and they spoke in tongues and prophesied.*

Later, some of the men were probably in the pastoral team of elders appointed by Paul (Acts 20) to shepherd the Ephesian community, which was to experience much hardship over the subsequent years. Happily, the Holy Spirit gave them power to stand, to endure and to testify. In many ways they were a model local church, but we cannot ignore the letter that the risen and ascended Jesus later instructed the apostle John to send 'To the angel of the church in Ephesus'. (See Revelation 2:1-7 where we read a number of commendations, but also this: 'You have forsaken the love you had at first. Consider how far you have fallen! Repent and do the things you did at first.') Their relationship with Jesus was not right and needed to be renewed. They needed to be filled anew, baptised afresh with the Holy Spirit. Earlier, Paul's letter to them had exhorted them:

> *Therefore do not be foolish, but understand what the Lord's will is. Do not get drunk on wine, which leads to debauchery. Instead, **be filled with the Spirit**, speaking to one another with psalms, hymns, and songs from the Spirit. Sing and make music from your heart to the Lord, always giving thanks to God the Father for everything, in the name of our Lord Jesus Christ. (Ephesians 5:17-21)*

On the basis of scanty, but significant, historical evidence we can assume that the Ephesian Christians heeded the warnings and exhortations they had received, and the Holy Spirit continued to work wonderfully in and through their community. During the second century AD Justin Martyr was converted at Ephesus, and he became a greatly blessed Christian philosopher and itinerant missionary. In the same century Ignatius of Antioch wrote a letter to the Ephesian church in which he expressed his appreciation of the community.

Paul's letter to the Ephesian Christians is packed full, on the one hand, of edifying doctrine, and on the other, of guidance concerning practical and holy Christian living. Just after the beginning of the letter he reminded them of the earlier action of the Spirit in their lives: 'When you believed [in Christ], you were marked in him with a seal, the promised Holy Spirit, who is a deposit guaranteeing our inheritance' (1:13-14). Towards the end of his message Paul again emphasises the importance of the Spirit exhorting the Ephesians to 'pray in the Spirit on all occasions with all kinds of prayers and requests' (6:18).

Accompanying signs

Whilst reading the accounts in Acts of the five recorded occasions when Christians received the baptism with the Holy-Spirit, our attention is caught by the mention of supernatural, spiritual signs that accompanied the Spirit's action. Here is brief summary:

The large group of worshipping disciples on the day of Pentecost: a sound like the blowing of a violent wind; tongues of fire; speaking in other tongues. The company of newly converted persons in Samaria: something that Simon (a sorcerer) 'saw' (maybe heard) and found intriguing. Saul: restoration of his sight. The people assembled at Cornelius' house: speaking in tongues. The group of believers at Ephesus: speaking in tongues and prophesying.

These accounts convey the impression of Holy Spirit workings that had a dynamic effect on the persons concerned and their entire beings, including their vocal capacities. Speaking in tongues is mentioned in three out of the five reports. Years later Paul, in his first letter to the Corinthian church, wrote, 'I thank God that I speak in tongues more than all of you' (14:18). Here he was writing about speaking in tongues in personal devotion, not in order to transmit a message to a church gathering (via interpretation). It could well be that he began to speak in tongues when he was filled with the Spirit as Ananias laid hands on him, but the text does not say so. As for the company in Samaria, whilst it seems that a sign, or signs, of supernatural nature were observed by Simon, there is no way, for us, of **knowing** what they were.

Today, and in the past, many have been powerfully blessed and equipped for service by a baptism with the Spirit accompanied by speaking in tongues. They have thereby discovered an expanded liberty in praise and worship, and a means of praying when words in their natural language have been difficult or impossible to find. Furthermore, the testimony of the early church (as found in Acts) and of the church since, is that the baptism with the Holy Spirit conveys power for testimony (Acts 1:8) and evangelistic zeal, a greatly enhanced assurance of salvation (particularly for persons of doubting personality), a confidence that all things are possible to him who believes, an open door to the reception of spiritual gifts and much more.

The question of 'accompanying signs' has long been a subject of different opinion, sometimes acute and divisive difference, and we have no desire at all to lead our readers into hot debate or unholy division. But the nettle must be grasped, and all who long for the Holy Spirit to work in them and through them, and their communities, need to search the scriptures in order to know God's mind on the matter.

Waiting or tarrying

On one occasion during the 40-day period following his resurrection, Jesus instructed his disciples to 'not leave

Jerusalem, but **wait** for the gift my Father promised, which you have heard me speak about. For John baptised with water, but in a few days you will be baptised with the Holy Spirit' (Acts 1:4-5). They did wait, they were expectant, united and worshipful, and they were baptised with the Spirit by the ascended Lord Jesus.

Since then, many Christians, individually and in groups, have waited ('tarried' in the KJV) in prayer before the Lord in order to receive the baptism with the Holy Spirit. For a very great many the outcome has been wonderful; the Spirit has come upon them with power. Others have waited and tarried but little has happened (or so it has seemed). Nevertheless, dear reader, please be attentive to the Spirit's leading; if you are led to wait before the Lord then please do so. It could be that God wants you to experience anew the cleansing power of Jesus' blood in order to prepare you for receiving more of the **Holy Spirit.**

We should note that none of the persons involved in the other accounts (in Acts) of Spirit baptism were instructed to wait; rather, it is apparent that other verbs of action were more relevant. We have in mind 'to thirst' (John 7:37-39), 'to ask' (Luke 11:9-13) and to receive (Acts 8:17). We are not called on to plead with a reluctant God, but to have a consuming longing for, to humbly and expectantly ask for and, with open heart and faith, accept the gift of our loving Father.

Laying on of hands

The ministry of laying on hands has an important role concerning the reception of the baptism with the Holy

Spirit. This ministry was present on three out of the five occasions described in the Book of Acts. In Samaria it was two apostles, Peter and John, who exercised this ministry; at Damascus it was a disciple, Ananias (who may also have been a prophet), who laid his hands on Saul; at Ephesus it was Saul, now the apostle Paul, who ministered in this way. The fact that Ananias was used in this way suggests that it is not a ministry which can only be practised by an apostle.

God uses this ministry today! Those who minister in this way need to wait on God for an anointing of the Spirit, and to exercise their role with discernment and grace, bearing in mind the attitude Paul certainly had in mind when writing to Timothy, 'Do not be hasty in the laying on of hands' (1 Timothy 5:22).

During the early church period, for some while thereafter, from time to time throughout the subsequent centuries and particularly since the beginning of the 20th century, many millions of Christians have experienced baptism with, or in, the Holy Spirit in the manner described in Acts. This has been and still is of vital importance for worldwide evangelism, for equipping the church of Jesus for all aspects of her life and ministry and for preparing her to be the bride of Christ.

4

Assurance

There are phrases that are frequently on the lips of all of us; two examples are, 'I'm sure' and 'I'm not sure'. Being assured, or not so being, are constantly of fundamental importance to our everyday living. Husband says, 'I'm not sure – what day is it?' Wife replies, 'You should be. It's Monday, the rubbish collection lorry has just passed!'

Maybe it would be nice to be sure about everything, but that is clearly not the lot of humans, limited as we are. Nevertheless, the Bible tells us that there are great matters concerning which God wants us to possess assurance, indeed full assurance, certainty and conviction. He wants us to be assured regarding our salvation, his will, his purposes, his love. We want this assurance, we need it, but how are we to acquire it?

Consider a baby, offspring of loving parents: it wakes, senses mother's presence, hears her voice, feels hunger or discomfort, cries out assuredly/insistently/expectantly, and a change and feed are rapidly on their way. Baby's assurance is partly intuitive and partly based on happy previous experience. And so on through life; events and relationships through 'baby's' life will either enhance, educate and mature the foundational assurance, or do the opposite. We have all experienced both enhancing and destructive influences which have tended to make of us a mixed bag insofar as confidence, trust, faith and assurance are concerned. This, coupled with our inherited sinful nature, implies that every one of us is in need of healing, rectification and re-construction, all of which God offers to us in his redemption purpose through Jesus Christ and his gift of the Holy Spirit. The Bible message of full salvation in Christ Jesus includes the healing and remedying of the damaged human condition in the area of assurance.

A baby may have no intellectual knowledge of assurance – that is, not in the way that an adult can have – but it is sure and certain that the tiniest of infants either experiences it or suffers from its absence. Parental love, presence, comfort, faithfulness, provision and ability combine to foster security and contented assurance. Father God manifests all these attributes to his children. Let us briefly explore biblical teaching on the matter.

Greek words

Plerophoreo: to be fully assured, convinced, persuaded, e.g. in Colossians 4:12, 'Epaphras . . . is always wrestling in prayer for you, that you may stand firm in all the will of God, mature and **fully assured**.'

The Greek word combines *pleros,* meaning 'full', with *phero,* 'to carry'.

Plerophoria: complete, conviction, full assurance, sure, e.g.:

Colossians 2:2: 'My [Paul's] goal is that they may . . . have the full riches of **complete** understanding, in order that they may know the mystery of God.'

1 Thessalonians 1:5: 'Our gospel came to you . . . with power, with the Holy Spirit and **deep conviction**.'

Hebrews 6:11: 'Show this same diligence to the very end, so that what you hope for may be **fully realised**' (or **assured**).

Hebrews 10:22: 'Let us draw near to God with a sincere heart and with the **full assurance** that faith brings.'

In English we have the word 'plethora', meaning an excess of something; it is of course impossible to have an excess of something that God gives in grace, in the present case, full assurance of faith.

Other texts which link Christian assurance to the work of the Holy Spirit

For those who are led by the Spirit of God are the children of God. The Spirit you received does not make you slaves, so that you live in fear again; rather, the Spirit you received brought about your adoption to sonship. And by him we cry, 'Abba, Father.' **The Spirit himself testifies with our spirit** *that we are God's children. Now if we are children, then we are heirs – heirs of God and co-heirs with Christ, if indeed we share in his sufferings in order that we may also share in his glory. (Romans 8:14-17)*

The word 'assurance' is not present in these lines but they are charged through and through with solid certainty and full assurance based on the truth that 'those who are in Christ Jesus' (8:1) are no longer under condemnation, they are born again, the Holy Spirit resides in them, they are sons of God and joint heirs with Jesus, their elder brother and Lord, provided they are willing to share in his sufferings. But Christians might ask, 'How does the Spirit testify to our spirit?' What is his method? What are the mechanics of his work?

Some would say that it is primarily by way of participation in the sacraments, particularly Holy Communion (Eucharist for many). Of these many find their assurance in the ecclesiastic system to which they adhere, and the sacerdotal authority (to absolve the sins of the penitent) that the system conveys on its priests. Others, whilst acknowledging the importance of the sacraments to the consolidation of faith and the strengthening of assurance, are dogmatic in their conviction that it is only by the simple acceptance of what Scripture says that true assurance of salvation comes to a believer's heart and mind.

Our position is that, as in all matters of faith, Scripture (the Bible) is the only basis for Christian assurance in all its aspects, including assurance of salvation, of knowing God (his person, his attributes and his will), and all other matters concerning godly living, and service to him and to our fellows. To this we must add that Christians, individually and collectively, are not left in isolation in their reading of Scripture or listening to biblical teaching. The Father, through the Son, has given the Holy Spirit, the Spirit of truth, to instruct (through Scripture, creation and revelation) and to testify, assure, confirm to everyone who, in penitence, places their trust in Jesus Christ the Saviour, that they are indeed accepted and born again; this equates to full assurance of salvation. The Spirit prompts believers to address God as Father, indeed as Abba; this is most blessed assurance!

> *Because you are his sons, God sent the Spirit of his Son into our hearts, the Spirit who calls out, 'Abba, Father.' So you are no longer a slave, but God's child; and since you are his child, God has made you also an heir. (Galatians 4:6-7)*

Here we discover that full assurance leads a believer to a dynamic awareness of the greatness of the inheritance he possesses; this in turn increases a believer's sense of responsibility and the cost of discipleship.

> *This salvation, which was first announced by the Lord, was confirmed to us by those who heard him. God also testified to it by signs, wonders and various miracles, and by gifts of the Holy Spirit distributed according to his will. (Hebrews 2:3-4)*

This passage plainly implies that throughout the period of Jesus' public ministry, and that of the early church, the oral teaching was attested to and confirmed by the miraculous, the visible supernatural actions of the Holy Spirit; this equated to the presence of much assurance within the church. The challenge to the 21st-century church is evident.

The disciples, the 120 including the womenfolk who had followed Jesus, were all fully persuaded that their Lord had risen from the dead. Most, perhaps all, had met with their risen Master, and they were all together on the day of Pentecost when the Holy Spirit descended upon and filled them. One of the consequences of this was that the assurance they had that Jesus had risen was powerfully confirmed; they now possessed the *plerophoreo/ plerophoria,* the full assurance that Jesus was alive that would make of them the company that shook the world.

The Holy Spirit is working in the same manner today. It was he who raised Jesus from the grave; Romans 1:4 says that the Son 'through the Spirit of holiness appointed the Son of God in power by his resurrection from the dead: Jesus Christ our Lord'. Paul also writes of 'the Spirit of him who raised Jesus from the dead' (Romans 8:11).

5
Testimony

Multitudes have borne testimony to the person and work of Jesus, and they have done so individually and collectively in many ways. From Old Testament times, through Jesus' lifetime, to the present day, much oral testimony has been rendered, but writing, music, workmanship and godly (sacrificial, generous, kindly) living, with much variety around these and other themes, have also been part of the rich tapestry of witness to Jesus' Lordship. God the Holy Spirit has lovingly inspired and powerfully employed all the testimony of the Master's disciples.

Looking back, I clearly recall the witness of my mother, of the Sunday school teachers (so patient and persevering in the face of my dislike of attending their classes), of village lads with whom I enjoyed strong bonds and shared what we believed were sound values, and later, after the family moved to a new location, of boys and young men who knew Jesus as Saviour and Lord. There were other means by which testimony to Jesus reached me, and the Spirit of God used them all; I became enthralled by the person of

Jesus and consumed by his achievements and teaching. This was the groundwork that led to my conversion. Testimony to Christ reached me in many ways, through many persons.

The Book of the Acts of the Apostles is about many important matters, one of the most obvious being testimony. This is not surprising for it begins by reporting Jesus' last word to his disciples, 'You will receive power when the Holy Spirit comes on you; and you will be my **witnesses** in Jerusalem, and in all Judea and Samaria, and to the ends of the earth' (Acts 1:8). After this final declaration Jesus ascended!

Thereafter, the account in Acts tells how testimony to Jesus, his death and resurrection grew and grew. Here is a short summary:

During the 10-day wait for Pentecost the apostles realised that their calling was to be witnesses of Jesus' resurrection (1:22).

On the day of Pentecost, filled with the Holy Spirit, they clearly and graciously testified to a crowd of Jewish pilgrims concerning Jesus and the essentials of the gospel, using Joel's prophecy (Joel 2:28-32) as their springboard (2:14-41).

Thereafter, there was much oral witness, and also testimony to Jesus and his power by way of healings, signs and wonders (4:30).

Sharing of possessions and unity were closely associated with powerful witness.

> *After they prayed, the place where they were meeting was shaken. And they were all filled with the Holy Spirit*

and spoke the word of God boldly. All the believers were one in heart and mind. No one claimed that any of their possessions was their own, but they shared everything they had. With great power the apostles continued to testify to the resurrection of the Lord Jesus. And God's grace was so powerfully at work in them all. (4:31-33)

From Jerusalem to Judea, on to Samaria, Syria, the Mediterranean coast, Asia Minor and parts of Europe, the testimony, inspired by the Holy Spirit, was always the same, centred on Jesus as the last verse of the book attests, 'Boldly and without hindrance he [Paul] preached the kingdom of God and taught about the Lord Jesus Christ' (Acts 28:31 NIV 1984).

The vital role of the Holy Spirit in Christian testimony

This was clearly explained by Jesus. Elsewhere we have taken note of the following citations, but we shall do well to give them further careful consideration:

John 15:26-27: 'When the Advocate comes, whom I will send to you from the Father – the Spirit of truth who goes out from the Father – **he will testify about me. And you also must testify.**'

John 16:13-15: 'He will speak only what he hears . . . the Spirit will receive from me what he will make known to you.'

Concerning the crucifixion and resurrection of Jesus, Peter and the other apostles said to the assembled Sanhedrin, 'We are witnesses of these things, **and so is the Holy Spirit**, whom God has given to those who obey him' (Acts 5:32).

Christians can confidently rely on the Holy Spirit to bear witness through them to Jesus and his redemptive work.

Some of the vehicles of Christian testimony
Art and workmanship

We, a small group of evangelical Christians visiting a village in the Belgian province of Walloon Brabant, called in on the local parish priest. After talking and praying together he showed us his workshop and some of the wrought-iron pieces he had made or was still working on. Many were simple but elegant and eloquent shapes of Christ on the cross. As testimony to our Saviour, they left us with a strong and lasting impression. Surely it pleases the Holy Spirit to speak by such testimonies about the sacrifice of Jesus and his love for the world.

Through the centuries Christians have used many art and craft forms to depict biblical events, stories and persons, with an overwhelming emphasis on the life and work of Jesus. Stained-glass works, usually in church windows, have been particularly influential, especially in Europe. Some stained-glass windows have won worldwide renown due to their beauty, intricacy, sheer size and dominance; e.g. the window in the South Transept of Chartres Cathedral, France. For our present purpose we would draw attention to the art works, usually of stained glass, known as Poor Man's Bibles. One is in Canterbury Cathedral, England; it dates from the 13th century and was constructed of fragments from, perhaps, two earlier windows. The initial purpose of a Poor Man's Bible was to illustrate Bible teachings for the benefit of a largely illiterate population. They still have a role, for we live in a day when most folk prefer the visual to the wordy! Broadly, their purpose is to show viewers 'The Way of Salvation' by illustrating two major biblical revelations: the message of mankind's sorrow, guilt and fear, and the coming day of judgment; the message of faith, hope and love brought to mankind by Jesus through his birth, life, death and resurrection, and God's love, his grace, his mercy and his glory.

The world has been enriched by the many magnificent paintings that famous and less well-known artists have produced. Today some of these do not have the impact they once enjoyed; we still admire their art, but for many of us they seem to have a religiosity and an ecclesiasticism that is very distant from contemporary living and vision. Two, out of probably many, timeless exceptions are well worth mentioning, or so it seems to us; they are:

'Ecce Homo'

'Ecce Homo' (Behold the Man) by Guido Reni (1575–1642) which is in London's National Gallery. It depicts the thorn-crowned head of Christ. The face, particularly the upward looking eyes, speak agony and suffering. We see something of 'The Man of Sorrows' and this makes for powerful testimony to Jesus presented by an artist known to have certain character deficiencies.

'The Angelus' (a devotional prayer, *Angelus Domini*, or 'The Angel of the Lord') by Jean-Francois Millet of the rural Brabazon school, on view in the Musée d'Orsay, Paris. Millet, himself the son of a peasant farmer, shows a young farming couple standing in a field at dusk, heads bowed in prayer and thanksgiving. A basket on the ground and two sacks on their wheelbarrow contain the day's crop of potatoes, and they are expressing their gratitude to the Giver. Another associated work of Millet, 'The Sowers', bears testimony to the broadcasting of the good seed of the Word, and a third, 'The Gleaners', to the end of harvest time and to meeting the needs of the poor.

'The Angelus' by Millet

In Exodus 31:1-11 we are told that the workforce that constructed the Tent of Meeting and the Ark of the Testimony was led by Bezalel, a craftsman 'filled . . . with the Spirit of God'. He was assisted by Oholiab and a team of skilled men, who may all have been equally equipped by the Holy Spirit. What a model for the church! Paul would certainly challenge us all, as he did Timothy, 'Do your best to present yourself to God as one approved, a worker who does not need to be ashamed and who correctly handles the word of truth' (2 Timothy 2:15). A building site needs skilled and highly skilled operatives, but also unskilled men, general labourers, who assist, carry, dig and so on. May we, whichever category we are in, do everything to the utmost of our ability and under the anointing of the Spirit. Thereby our lives will testify of Jesus.

Priscilla, Aquila and Paul were all tent makers by trade, and earned their living thereby. Maybe they were highly skilled, maybe not, but we can be assured that the Holy Spirit accompanied their manual labours just as much as he did their oral testimony and teaching. Today, Christian witness is expressed through a wide range of art forms, ranging from the simple to the complex, e.g. flannelgraphs to floral designs, puppetry to ventriloquism, EvangeCubes[11] to animated story telling.

It is evident that the Lord requires that all his disciples carry out their daily tasks to the very best of their ability and in a gracious and humble manner. The Holy Spirit is our ever-present help, and he enables us to render faithful testimony to our Lord and Saviour in the areas of work and leisure.

A note of warning: there are professions, jobs, ways of earning a living which do not comply with biblical ethical

---

11. The EvangeCube is a portable evangelism tool, made up of a number of pictures on a cube that can be used to explain the gospel message.

criteria; we offend the Holy Spirit when we engage in such. Furthermore, and often more difficult to cope with, many Christians find that, however worthwhile, useful or necessary their profession is, temptation comes along to act in an unchristian, unethical manner. If we are walking in the Spirit he will always clearly show us what we should do. To obey may be painful (for others as well as us), but the price should be paid. When it is, the Spirit assures peace of heart and conscience, and the testimony rendered is certainly pleasing to Jesus.

Music and song

Music and song, very present in Scripture, have always been means by which the Holy Spirit has enabled believers to testify of Jesus. Multitudes have heard and received testimony to Christ whilst listening to, or taking part in, a production of Handel's 'Messiah', with its well-chosen Bible lyrics and uplifting music, a presentation of contemporary gospel music, the stirring heartfelt congregational singing of hymns and songs by Isaac Watts, Charles Wesley, Ira D. Sankey, Darlene Zschech, Keith and Kristyn Getty or the recollection of singing 'Jesus loves me' as a way of saying 'sleep well' to one's children.

Holy Spirit-anointed music and singing have, no doubt, been an integral part of testimony to Jesus since before Paul wrote to the Ephesians, 'Be filled with the Spirit, speaking to one another with psalms, hymns and songs from the Spirit. Sing and make music from your heart to the Lord' (Ephesians 5:18-19). By so doing believers have walked in the footsteps of harp-playing David, the shepherd king, and the singing sons of Korah.

Most of us feel unable to either compose music or write lyrics, but we love to worship and give testimony to our Lord using the work of others. Samuel Crossman wrote these words in 1664, and the tune 'Love Unknown' composed much later by John Ireland hugely contributed to its popular appeal:

> *My song is love unknown–*
> *my Saviour's love to me;*
> *love to the loveless shown,*
> *that they might lovely be.*
> *Oh, who am I, that for my sake*
> *my Lord should take frail flesh and die?*[12]

Hans Christian Andersen wrote, 'Where words fail, music speaks.'[13]

Corporeal expression

By this phrase many may immediately think of dance, or something similar, and there should be no doubt that the Holy Spirit can use this form of expression to convey testimony to Jesus and to what he wants to be to people. Spirit-anointed dance says to onlookers, 'Come and join us and share in the joy of the Lord!' However, there are many other less sophisticated, everyday and easy-to-practice physical gestures/expressions that the Spirit wants to inspire and use as testimony, e.g.: the right hand of fellowship (Galatians 2:9), as a sign of unity and agreement;

---

12. Samuel Crossman (1664), 'My song is love unknown', https://hymnary.org/text/my_song_is_love_unknown (accessed 26.3.24).
13. Hans Christian Andersen, 1805–1875, https://www.goodreads.com/quotes/90636-where-words-fail-music-speaks (accessed 26.3.24).

the extended helping hand, 'Taking him by the right hand, he helped him up [the crippled beggar]' (Acts 3:7).

A smile that says, 'We're equals, and I want you to know that I appreciate you.'

A gesture that says, 'After you!'

Many simple gestures have opened the way to friendship and to a mutually enhancing relationship.

Simple service

Experience shows that the Holy Spirit delights in using the loving and diligent accomplishment of simple tasks as testimony.

Elsewhere we have written about Lawrence, a 17th-century Carmelite lay brother who spent much of his day in his community's kitchen cleaning the pots and pans. He worked well and joyfully, becoming constantly aware of God's nearness; his precious little book *The Practice of the Presence of God*,[14] compiled after his death by Father Joseph de Beaufort, has blessed many throughout succeeding generations.

Stephen, and six others, were chosen by the Christians at Jerusalem to look after the welfare of the Hellenistic Jewish widows, their principal task being to 'wait on tables' (see Acts 6). The service rendered was simple in principle, but certainly required firmness, impartiality and love for the persons waited on. We note that Stephen was 'a man full

---

14. Brother Lawrence, The Practice of the Presence of God (London: Hodder & Stoughton, 1981).

of faith and of the Holy Spirit', very probably the six others too. No Christian service is too simple to not necessitate the assistance of the Holy Spirit. In Stephen's case it seems that the task he undertook within the community was part of the Lord's preparation of his servant for public and very costly ministry (see further comment below).

Written testimony

Peter, Paul, John, James, Jude and, presumably, many others of the early church era, were great letter writers; that was one of the most effective means for them to testify. Some of their letters were included in the biblical canon and have powerfully testified to billions; the Holy Spirit has never failed to speak of Jesus to their readers.

Today we have the Scriptures, in many languages, and they are the writings that the Spirit particularly privileges for witness concerning Jesus. Furthermore, a vast amount of other literature also exists which bears effective, heartfelt testimony to the Saviour. The material support for all this literature has varied from papyrus to paper, from clay tablet to hard disc and from billboards to (best of all) 'tablets of human hearts'. These all appear to be fragile, but time has shown that most have proved to be very durable, e.g. the ancient biblical manuscripts and the precious documents, books and testaments that libraries and families have conserved for generations. We might wonder whether our rapidly evolving and changing age will succeed equally well in the area of conservation?

It is good to know that presently there are a number of missions which major on the propagation of the gospel by means of the printed page; one is the Every Home for Christ mission, which is present in very many countries and seeks to concentrate on evangelising the hitherto unreached.

A tract was one of the several forms of testimony that led me to know Jesus; it cited Romans 7:18, 'I know that good itself does not dwell in me.' Reading these words of Paul brought me into deep conviction of sin, and a short while later, just after I had accepted Jesus as my Saviour and Lord, a Christian friend pointed me to verses 24-25 of the same chapter, 'What a wretched man I am! Who will rescue me from this body that is subject to death? Thanks be to God, who delivers me through Jesus Christ our Lord!' By this outburst of gratitude Paul explains that he came to understand that the deliverance he had longed for, but was powerless to achieve, was freely available to him in Christ. What a testimony! I am very grateful that Paul wrote it.

Many evangelicals are also engaged in more modern means of communication, such as social media. However, we must add a note of caution about the potential harmful misuse of social media. Indeed, we are all frequently informed by TV or radio of dreadful crimes involving similar misuse. Consequently, we suggest that Christian communities would do well to support governmental measures which have the intent of achieving a major transformation to the ways in which social media and its equipment can or cannot be used.

Oral testimony

Reports of oral testimony in the Book of Acts are abundant and, in many instances, detailed. They include public proclamation, one-on-one conversations, encounters with small groups, defence statements before religious and civic authorities, explanations to persons who had witnessed miracles, speaking in synagogues, houses, palaces and prisons, and to crew and passengers of a vessel about to be shipwrecked.

Let us take a more detailed look at just one person who bravely testified openly and orally knowing full well that he was putting his life at risk. We have already noted how Stephen rendered clear and kindly testimony to his Lord through his service to the poor widows at Jerusalem. Then his work and testimony went public; the dynamic and rapidly evolving story is related in Acts, from 6:8 to the end of chapter 7.

> *Now Stephen, a man full of God's grace and power, performed great wonders and signs among the people. Opposition arose, however, from members of the Synagogue of the Freedmen (as it was called) – Jews of Cyrene and Alexandria as well as the provinces of Cilicia and Asia – who began to argue with Stephen. But they could not stand up against* **the wisdom the Spirit gave him as he spoke**.

We can see here parallels to Jesus' course through the two to three years of his public ministry, and then, for Stephen, events took on a much darker turn, just as they did for Stephen's Master. False accusations, orchestrated by the Sanhedrin, and stirred up anger were directed at the young man, and the high priest asked him, 'Are these charges true?' Stephen, in contrast to Jesus, delivered a lengthy defence, concluding with this accusation and coupled with a testimony to Jesus.

> *You stiff-necked people! Your hearts and ears are still uncircumcised. You are just like your ancestors: you always resist the Holy Spirit! Was there ever a prophet your ancestors did not persecute? They even killed those who predicted the coming of the Righteous One. And now you have betrayed and murdered him – you who have received the law that was given through angels but have not obeyed it. (Acts 7:51-53)*

For Stephen the consequence to his forthright testimony was that his adversaries:

> *Gnashed their teeth at him. But Stephen, full of the Holy Spirit, looked up to heaven and saw the glory of God, and Jesus standing at the right hand of God. 'Look,' he said, 'I see heaven open and the Son of Man standing at the right hand of God.' At this they covered their ears and, yelling at the top of their voices, they all rushed at him, dragged him out of the city and began to stone him. Meanwhile, the witnesses laid their coats at the feet of a young man named Saul. While they were stoning him, Stephen prayed, 'Lord Jesus, receive my spirit.' Then he fell on his knees and cried out, 'Lord, do not hold this sin against them.' When he had said this, he fell asleep. And Saul approved of their killing him. (Acts 7:54-8:1)*

Stephen came to be known as the *Protomartyr.*

One wonders how many Christians, since Stephen, have similarly rendered testimony to Jesus. Is it happening somewhere in the world today? Certainly Christians in such circumstances have found great comfort in the advice

Jesus gave to his disciples, 'Whenever you are arrested and brought to trial, do not worry beforehand about what to say. Just say whatever is given you at the time, **for it is not you speaking, but the Holy Spirit**' (Mark 13:11).

Oral testimony can be very costly, in the family, in a friendship, the classroom, the workplace, the neighbourhood, and within a religious, political or philosophical group. Christian testifiers need the power and presence of the Holy Spirit.

Paul depended totally on the Spirit's power. To the Corinthian Christians he wrote,

> *I proclaimed to you the testimony about God . . . My message and my preaching were not with wise and persuasive words, but with a demonstration of the Spirit's power, so that your faith might not rest on human wisdom, but on God's power . . . The kingdom of God is **not a matter of talk but of power**. (1 Corinthians 2:1-5; 4:20)*

Words and actions are excellent vehicles, but to be effective they must be accompanied by the power of the Spirit.

Paul, Silas and Timothy stayed a very short while at Thessalonica, during which they were enabled to effectively communicate the gospel (the story is related in Acts 17). Some time later they wrote to the young local church:

> *Our gospel came to you **not simply with words but also with power, with the Holy Spirit and deep conviction** . . . for you welcomed the message in the midst of severe suffering with the joy given by the Holy Spirit. And so you became a model. (1 Thessalonians 1:5-7)*

Perhaps the most persuasive form of testimony
The unity of believers: Jesus says,

> My prayer is not for them alone. I pray also for those who will believe in me through their message, **that all of them may be one**, Father, just as you are in me and I am in you. May they also be in us so **that the world may believe** that you have sent me. (John 17:20-21)

Unity comes about when Christians are 'all together in one place', united in spirit, in the Spirit, in Jesus. Only then can all that divides Christians be removed – cultural, denominational, generational and doctrinal obstacles. Do readers have relevant testimonies to share?

Based on unity believers are able to credibly and convincingly proclaim, 'The word of faith . . . and the good news' and, best of all, to confess openly, 'Jesus is Lord!' (see Romans 10:8-17).

God's testimony to Israel and the church

God had brought Israel out of Egypt; he had redeemed his people. Through his servant Moses he had made a covenant with them. Then, as testimony (confirmation and witness) to his mighty work, he commanded the construction of the Tent of the Testimony (the Tabernacle) with as central feature, the Ark of the Testimony (Covenant). The Ark was a gold-covered chest of acacia wood into which were placed the three items which were to bear constant covenant testimony to Israel:

- the two tablets on which the finger of God had inscribed the Ten Commandments (Exodus 40:20); God's word to redeemed Israel;

- a gold jar containing manna (Hebrews 9:4), a reminder to the people of God's never-failing provision of food throughout their 40-year-long wanderings in the Sinai desert;
- Aaron's staff, representing the house of Levi, which, alone out of the 12 staffs by which each of the 12 Israelite tribes were represented, had sprouted, budded and blossomed, thereby testifying to all Israel that Levi was the tribe chosen for priesthood (Numbers 17 and Hebrews 9:4).

In the context of the New Covenant, God's testimony to the church is:

- his Word incarnate, Jesus (the Word made flesh), and written (in scripture and on human hearts);
- his great faithfulness in meeting our material, moral and spiritual needs (Philippians 4:19);
- we, every one of Jesus' disciples, living and flowering, are his chosen and appointed priesthood (1 Peter 2:4-5).

And the Holy Spirit testifies to our spirits that this is so!

It is the Spirit who testifies,
because the Spirit is the truth.
(1 John 5:6)

6

Prayer and Worship

Maybe there are exceptions, but people everywhere and at all times have wanted to pray to a deity, an object of worship, a power or a force greater and higher than themselves. Humans want to worship and are conscious of a need for help from outside of humanity. Both the Old and the New Testaments contain a large volume of texts on the matter – teaching, exhortations and examples of prayer. We can read the prayers of prophets, priests, kings, disciples, the persecuted, the proud, the humble, the sick, the dying and lots more. Of the supplications made to the Lord God some were accepted, others not.

Many in Bible days, and today, have difficulty in knowing how to pray. That was how Jesus' 12 disciples felt, so they asked the Master to teach them how. He responded by teaching them the prayer we know as 'The Lord's Prayer' (Luke 11:1-4; Matthew 6:9-13). He taught them to pray, as he himself did, that is to his and their heavenly Father. They also had the privilege of observing Jesus praying, and even on a few important occasions, of hearing the words he used, e.g. after the last supper (John 17), in the Garden of Gethsemane (Matthew 26:36-44), and when he was on the cross (Matthew 27:46; Luke 23:34).

All-important though they are we will not attempt to write further concerning Jesus' teaching and example, for our subject is the Holy Spirit and prayer. Jesus and the Holy Spirit are of course in complete harmony on this as they are on all other matters. Jesus said to his disciples, 'If you love me, keep my commandments. And I will ask [pray] the Father, and he will give you another advocate to help you and be with you for ever – the Spirit of truth' (John 14:15-17). The Father wonderfully answered the prayer of his Son. Furthermore, Jesus encouraged us to pray the Father that he give us the Holy Spirit (Luke 11:13).

Perhaps the most important help that the Spirit gives regarding prayer is to bring our attention to, or remind us of, and consequently enable us to assimilate, all that Jesus taught and practised on the matter.

A person born of the Spirit and the Word, i.e. a born-again person, delights in their filial relationship to God, and expresses this in prayer to the Father. Galatians 4:6 puts it this way: 'Because you are his sons, God sent the Spirit of his Son into our hearts, the Spirit who calls out, *"Abba, Father."*' As sons we are also heirs! The Holy Spirit inspires filial worship prayer. How good it is to **listen to and share in the prayer of a Christian expressing his love and gratitude to his Father God.** Some have not had a good relationship with their natural father but are overjoyed by all that they are discovering in their newly found child relationship to God and delight in addressing the Almighty as Father. Others do have a loving relationship with their natural father, and this is the springboard from which they plunge into an ever-deeper communion with their heavenly Father; the worship prayer of each is 'Abba, Father'.

The ministry of the Word, whether it be in edification or evangelism, is wonderfully effective when delivered in an atmosphere of Holy Spirit-anointed prayer. Acts 4 tells us that, after their release from the custody of the Sanhedrin, the apostles Peter and John went back to their fellow believers, and they all prayed together. All were under an anointing of the Spirit; in prayer they quoted scripture (Psalm 2) and added,

> 'Now, Lord, consider their [Herod, Pontius Pilate, the Gentiles and Israelites in Jerusalem] threats and enable your servants to speak your word with great boldness. Stretch out your hand to heal and perform signs and wonders through the name of your holy servant Jesus.' After they prayed, the place where they were meeting was shaken. And they were all filled with the Holy Spirit and spoke the word of God boldly. (Acts 4:29-31)

This incident is an example of the Holy Spirit being both the inspirer of prayer to the Father (the Sovereign Lord) and the substance of the answer that the Father gave.

We will now look at a few texts which enlighten us regarding the help the Spirit gives in the matter of prayer.

Ephesians 6:18-19

Paul is reaching the end of his message to the Christians at Ephesus. He has written on a number of weighty matters, including: the supremacy and majesty of Jesus Christ; the wonder that the church, the body of Christ, is; two expressions of prayer for his readers; the ministry gifts that the ascended Christ gives to the church; family life; and the spiritual and moral armour that Christians need to put on. Paul's teaching is so wide ranging and complete that we can conclude that if the initial recipients, and we today, were to fully appropriate all the materiel and put into practice every recommendation, we would be in a revival situation. Now, in order to ensure that such might be the case, Paul writes, '**Pray in the Spirit** on all occasions with all kinds of prayers and requests. With this in mind, be alert and always keep on praying for all the Lord's people. Pray also for me . . .'

What does praying in the Spirit imply? We are incapable of responding adequately to the question, but the implications must include being in tune, in harmony, with the Spirit who is holy, pure, patient, persevering, powerful and full of love and compassion. He, like Jesus, gets alongside us, indeed he indwells us for we are his temple; he pours his graces into us, and he enables us to formulate requests that accord with the Father's will; he ensures that we don't forget to offer praise and thanksgiving when making requests. The Believers' prayer recorded in Acts 4, mentioned earlier, is a model of prayer 'in the Spirit'.

Romans 8:26-27

In verses 22-25 Paul has explained that the pains (occasioning inner groans) that believers experience in this world whilst awaiting the 'redemption of their bodies', are alleviated by the blessed hope (certainty) of that coming redemption. He moves on to write, 'In the same way, the Spirit helps us in our weakness. We do not know what we ought to pray for, but **the Spirit himself intercedes** for us through wordless groans. And he who searches our hearts knows the mind of the Spirit, because the Spirit intercedes for God's people in accordance with the will of God.'

Jesus intercedes for us, and so does the Holy Spirit.

We are all weak in many respects, particularly, you may agree, in the matter of prayer; but it is so good to be told that the Holy Spirit helps us in our weakness. So let the weak say, 'I am strong'! And what ought we to pray for? We probably know what we want, and what we want to pray for! But what **ought** we to pray for? That which is the will of God is the easy answer, and the Scriptures speak of many subjects that accord with God's will. Nevertheless, there are matters that figure large in our lives, which are important to us and to others, but we find ourselves perplexed as to whether we ought to make them matters of prayer, and, if we do, in what way should we bring them to God. However, there are often times when light shines into our uncertainty, or our lack of discernment, and with gratitude we give ourselves to enlightened intercession. There are other times when we feel more and more concerned, burdened, for a person, about an issue, for a manifestation of God's power, but we are uncertain, or ignorant, as to how we ought to pray. In such circumstances, Paul writes, 'The Spirit himself intercedes for us through wordless groans,' or as the NIV 1984 puts it, 'groans that words cannot express'. This is immensely strengthening. Jesus prays for us (Hebrews 7:25), the Holy Spirit too! Furthermore, the Spirit prays through us for others and for ourselves. There are times when we are unable to think of words with which to express our prayer; we are conscious of deep yearnings, longings, pains, burdens within; the text groups these as 'wordless groans'.

Some have experienced, individually or in a group, that deep burdened prayer in tongues has been like a groaning. No doubt others can testify differently concerning the manner in which the Spirit has prayed for them and through them. We are on holy ground here and must therefore stop using words in an attempt to describe the indescribable. Let us be practical and fraternal and simply do all that we can to encourage our communities to open up to all that the Spirit longs to pray through and for God's people.

Zechariah 12:10

'I [the Lord] will pour out on the house of David and the inhabitants of Jerusalem a spirit of grace and supplication. They will look on me, the one they have pierced, and they will mourn for him.' We prefer the alternative translation, 'the Spirit of grace' (NKJV)! The picture here is of the Jewish people becoming deeply aware of their sin; they, and their Gentile masters, had unjustly 'pierced' the Son of God (John 19:34-37), and they were to know a profound sense of wrongdoing; they would mourn for him. Then the Holy Spirit would come to their aid, bringing grace and stimulating prayers of supplication, cries for mercy, pardon and restoration. On the day of Pentecost this prophetic picture began to be fulfilled. The Spirit of grace and supplication came upon many Jews; about three thousand became disciples of the one they had pierced. The further fulfilment of the prophecy is ongoing; the Holy Spirit is revealing Jesus, the Messiah, to 'the house of David and the inhabitants of Jerusalem'.

Jude 20-21

'But you, dear friends, by building yourselves up in your most holy faith and praying in the Holy Spirit, keep yourselves in God's love.' This is a plain resume of our subject. The more we are built up the more we will pray; more exactly, the more we will give place to praying in the Holy Spirit. Matthew Henry wrote, 'Prayer is the nurse of faith. Our prayer is then most likely to prevail when we pray in the Holy Ghost, under his guidance and influence.'[15]

Worship

Worship is always adoration, appreciation, acclamation, recognition of sovereignty and pre-eminence, thanksgiving and prayer; this does not necessarily imply prayer in the usual sense, i.e. **words** of adoration that we understand addressed to God. Worship can simply be a God-centred attitude of heart and mind, a corporeally expressed giving of glory to God, an act of compassion motivated by love for God and neighbour or the playing of a musical instrument in praise to Father, Son and Holy Spirit. You probably have other ideas along these lines.

A well-known source (the Westminster Shorter Catechism) tells us that the first duty and privilege ('chief end')[16] of mankind is to glorify God and enjoy him forever. If we persevere and progress in the glorifying of our Creator we are progressing in our worship and enjoyment of him; expressed along the lines of Jesus' discourse with a Samaritan lady, we recognise that 'God is spirit [Spirit], and his worshippers must worship in the Spirit and in truth' (John 4:24). We cannot resist the alternative translations

---

15. *Matthew Henry's Commentary on the Whole Bible, Complete and Unabridged in One Volume* (Peabody MA: Hendrickson Publishers, 1991), p.2463.
16. Westminster Shorter Catechism, https://www.westminsterconfession.org/resources/confessional-standards/the-westminster-shorter-catechism/ (accessed 21.4.24).

for surely Jesus wanted the woman, and us, to understand the essential role of the Holy Spirit in worship.

As a child I spent much time in the Soar Valley meadows in central Leicestershire, most often in the company of other pleasure- and adventure-seeking village lads. Those were idyllic times! It often rained in our area, but I remember, almost exclusively, the warm sunshine-blessed days, especially those of the spring hay-making season. The buzz of insects, the songs of indigenous and migrating birds, the scent of drying hay, the gentle south-westerly breezes moving on the puffy white-light grey clouds, the river winding its lazy way northwards and the simple peels of bells reaching us from nearby village churches calling, my mother had told me, to 'Come to church'. No doubt some folk heeded the call, but not we boys, not directly anyway! I hear those bells whilst writing these lines; now they say, 'Come and worship', so I do! I still don't fully understand the mechanism, but I hear the call and feel the pull of the Spirit; you too no doubt, as Psalm 100 says we want to worship the Lord with gladness. This psalm and others, such as Psalm 22:22-31, call upon 'all the earth' to render homage to the Lord in anticipation of the day when 'all the ends of the earth will remember and turn to the Lord, and all the families of the nations will bow down before him, for dominion belongs to the Lord and he rules over the nations'. Holy Spirit energised bells are peeling out to people everywhere to turn to Christ in humble contrition and faith in order to worship Father, Son and Spirit in the splendour (beauty) of his holiness.

For our worship to be acceptable to God it '**must [be]** in the Spirit and in truth'. Jesus is 'the truth' (John 14:6); he is truth incarnate, expressed by what he is, what he says, and what he does. It is he who must motivate and be the subject of our worship. All falsehood and self-centredness must be excluded. We need help! This comes to us in the person of the Holy Spirit, he who reveals Jesus to us, helps us to understand our Master and all that he taught, guides us into truth and enables us to do that which, without his aid, we cannot do, i.e. worship God in Spirit and in truth.

The teaching Jesus shared with the Samaritan seems to imply that the place of worship, maybe the time too, plus a number of other factors we can all think of, are of secondary importance. It is Spirit and truth that count.

Personal, alone with God, worship is a wonderful privilege which, for the most part, is problem free. It could be that we use passages of scripture (truth) as a guide, or a document on prayer and worship, or an object such as a flower or a painting, a humble place that we appreciate as a sanctuary, a corner of our garden or a local park. Our hearts and minds are open and receptive to truth, and the Spirit moves us to worship. In his personal devotions the apostle Paul spoke in tongues: 'I thank God that I speak in tongues more than all of you' (1 Corinthians 14:18). The text seems to suggest that he was not referring to his use of tongues in corporate worship, but to his personal devotions. We understand that by his speaking to God in tongues his communion with the Lord was greatly enriched. It seems probable that he began speaking in tongues when he was 'filled with the Holy Spirit' whilst Ananias prayed with him (Acts 9:17). Thereafter, it would seem, he continued to pray and worship in tongues, particularly when alone with his Lord. Here we hasten to note that Paul teaches us that speaking in tongues in this personal way is not the same as conveying a message from God to a community of Christians via the exercise of the twin spiritual gifts of tongues and interpretation. We hope that believers reading this will feel encouraged to be receptive to the infilling of the Holy Spirit with the accompanying spiritual sign of tongues.

Corporate worship is certainly a very necessary and natural part of Christian living. We are a body, a temple, and worship is the normal, appreciated and cherished activity in which we join together with others who love the Lord. Here we acknowledge that, for a wide range of reasons, some Christians are not at ease in this area. It is not for us to endeavour to address these difficulties, except by saying that the Holy Spirit longs to come to our aid.

Our experiences of corporate worship may be in small groups, numbering two persons upwards, or larger gatherings. The character and organisation of the worship will in part be determined by such factors as ecclesiastical traditions and doctrinal positions, language, musical preference, our age, our relationships with the other worshippers and, most importantly, the closeness or otherwise of our walk with Jesus. The most widely practised forms of worship include liturgical, freestyle, entirely conducted from 'the front' by clergy or other leaders and 'open to all present to participate individually in various ways'. Does the Holy Spirit favour any particular form? We have no mandate to suggest an answer! All Christian communities have a duty to seek the Spirit's guidance in the matter and thus to keep in step with the Spirit. Time moves on and so must we, being led by the Spirit. May we in this so central issue of worship move on, being sensitive to cultural, social and ethnic changes in our locality, and the constantly evolving aspirations of our young people, not forgetting our 'seniors', some of whom find change difficult to digest.

We have written a few lines on the place for tongues in personal prayer and worship, and wish now to share a testimony concerning praying and singing in tongues in corporate worship. A few years ago a friend, a member of a Brethren denomination, reminded my wife and me of a visit he paid to the church in Anderlecht, Brussels, where we were in fellowship. He cherished the memories he had of this worship service: a lady received a prophetic message from the Lord and delivered it under the inspiration of the Holy Spirit; the congregation responded wholeheartedly in harmonious praise and worship; many moved on into praying and singing in tongues. Our friend was deeply touched and he testified to us of having felt that he was in heaven.

This was not a unique or isolated incident. Today, throughout the world, many communities experience such precious times of communion with their Lord.

We want to be careful not to convey the impression that we believe worship in the Spirit to necessitate Pentecostal style manifestations; this of course is not so. However, we take the liberty of encouraging our non-Pentecostal readers to be open minded to the Holy Spirit in the matter of worship. None of us should shut off to a worship dimension simply because it is not customary in our usual circle. Surely, we all have a lot to learn and new avenues to walk. There are depths and challenges to be discovered in Acts and the Letters which can take us upwards in the sphere of worship whilst taking us lower, ever lower at the feet of Jesus. We remember the womenfolk who, having left the empty tomb, suddenly met Jesus and 'they came to him, clasped his feet and worshipped him' (Matthew 28:9).

Music in worship

The place accorded to music in worship is clearly set out in scripture; the titles to many of the psalms indicate the instruments which usually accompanied their singing; David glorified God whilst playing an instrument, by singing to him and by dancing before him; three great choirs composed of Levites led Israel in worship; and the New Testament tells us how important singing and music are in Christian worship.

> *Be filled with the Spirit, speaking to one another with psalms, hymns and songs from the Spirit. Sing and make music from your heart to the Lord, always giving thanks to God the Father for everything, in the name of our Lord Jesus Christ. (Ephesians 5:18-20)*

We take note of the strong link between 'filled with the Spirit' and worship (see also Colossians 3:16). What wonderful encouragement for Christian musicians, singers and singing congregations to heed the exhortation to be filled with the Spirit.

Whether your instrument be a simple tambourine, a complex and awe-inspiring pipe organ or a croaky voice, please play it or use it, under the inspiration and control of the Spirit, to glorify the Lord our God.

Corporeal expression

Some Christians greatly enjoy worshipping in a corporeally expressive manner; some do so with exuberance, others quietly and calmly. Others are greatly put off by all of this nature! Much depends on what our home community or denomination consider acceptable, and culture, language, temperament and degree of religious freedom are all factors that determine the character of our corporeal expression.

There are still denominations that discourage, in some cases repress, any display of emotion and physical expression in worship; there are others that have had these characteristics in the past and are now trying to move on into a freer and more expressive mode. Change doesn't often come easily or rapidly. No doubt much could be said and written on the subject; there are cultural, doctrinal, psychological and spiritual considerations which must be addressed. Rocking the boat is unlikely to help; better by far to wait on the Lord for a visitation of the Holy Spirit. After Jesus' ascension the 120 disciples did this, and after a ten-day wait the Spirit descended upon them and they worshipped. The worship was vocal: they declared the wonders of God in the several tongues of the pilgrims present in Jerusalem. The worship was also corporeal: they comported themselves as if they had drunk too much wine.

Let us with grace and good sense make progress in worship in our communities. The Spirit and the Word will guide us. Our Bibles tell us that our capacity for vocal expression is important in worship: praying, praising, shouting, singing, whispering, laughing, weeping. We can also worship corporeally, that is with our bodies: smiling, dancing, waving (wave offerings), clapping, bowing down, prostrating.

The Christian's privilege and principal role

Philippians 3:3: 'It is we who are the circumcision, **we who worship by the Spirit of God**, who glory in Christ Jesus, and put no confidence in the flesh' (NIV 1984).

How far do we want to go?

In its original sense the Hebrew for the verb 'to worship' means 'to prostrate oneself on the ground'.

7

Circumcision of the Heart by the Spirit

Physical circumcision, without anaesthesia, must be a very painful business, the thought of which makes most men shudder. Notwithstanding, throughout known history and in a number of cultures, many millions of men and small boys have been subjected to the ordeal, the most common motivation being religious. The practice which particularly interests Christians is that inaugurated by God himself; this he did as an integral part of the covenant he made with 99-year-old Abram whose only child at the time was Ishmael, then aged 13. Genesis chapter 17 gives us the full story of the making, the content and the purpose of the covenant.

The Lord appeared to Abram and said, 'I am God Almighty [*El-Shaddai*]; walk before me faithfully and be blameless. Then I will make my covenant between me and you and will greatly increase your numbers' (Genesis 17:1-2). Previously the Lord had made promises (commitments) to Abram (see Genesis 12:2-3, 13:14-16, 15:4-5); now he confirms these in a covenant (Genesis 17:1-2), the Hebrew word being *berit* meaning 'to fetter', which helps us to understand the binding character of the commitment. Hearing the Lord's declaration Abram fell face down (v.3), and God said to him, 'As for me, this is my covenant with you: you will be the father of many nations' (v.4). So from an already amazing promise to greatly increase his numbers God now covenants with Abram that he will be the father of many nations; a prodigious progeny is God's promise to his servant, and this leads on to an appropriate change of name for the recipient:.

> *No longer will you be called Abram [exalted father]; your name will be Abraham [father of many], for I have made you a father of many nations. I will make you very fruitful; I will make nations of you, and kings will come from you. I will establish my covenant as an everlasting covenant between me and you and your descendants after you for the generations to come, to be your God and the God of your descendants after you. The whole land of Canaan, where you now reside as a foreigner, I will give . . . to you and your descendants after you; and I will be their God. (v.5-8)*

The continuation of the Genesis account is the part that particularly concerns us:

> *Then God said to Abraham, 'As for you, you must keep my covenant, you and your descendants after you for the generations to come. This is my covenant with you and your descendants after you, the covenant you are to keep: every male among you shall be circumcised.*

You are to undergo circumcision, and it will be the sign of the covenant between me and you. (v.9-11)

The account continues with God explaining in detail who were to be included in the term 'every male', God promising that Sarah, Abraham's wife, would give birth to a son whose name was to be Isaac and that Ishmael, Abraham's son by Hagar, Sarah's slave, would be blessed and fruitful and that his descendants would become a 'great nation'. And then, when God had left him, 'Abraham took his son Ishmael and all those born in his household or bought with his money, every male in his household, and circumcised them, as God told him' (v.23). Trying to imagine what went on that day is a worthwhile exercise! The men, youths and adolescents would each have right to an explanation for what they were required to undergo, some would need to have their courage bolstered and all would have to bear the pain with no means of alleviating it; that is to say no means of which today's readers are made aware. 'Every male in Abraham's household, including those born in his household or bought from a foreigner, was circumcised with him' (v.27).

Circumcision became the physical sign of identification for Jews, and later for Muslims.

Some 2,000 years later

The apostle Paul included a revolutionary statement on the subject of Jewish identity in his letter to the Christian community at Rome. It reads:

A person is not a Jew who is one only outwardly, nor is circumcision merely outward and physical. No, a person is a Jew who is one inwardly; and circumcision is circumcision of the heart, by the Spirit, not by the written code. Such a person's praise is not from other people, but from God. (Romans 2:28-29)

In the spiritual sense implied by the text this scripture tells us that Jewish identity is not determined by whether or not a man has been circumcised, as required by the Abrahamic covenant, or by his being a descendant of Abraham through Isaac. Rather it is dependent on the New Covenant inaugurated by Jesus Christ, and the sign of its implementation is not physical circumcision but a spiritual and moral operation on the innermost part of a person, described as 'circumcision of the heart, by the Spirit'. The strong implication, especially when other New Testament passages are taken into consideration, is that this New Covenant circumcision is for all believers, female and male, no matter which ethnic group they belong to, or whatever their civic or social status might be. This is borne out by:

Colossians 2:1-12, particularly 10-12:

In Christ you have been brought to fullness. He is the head over every power and authority. In him you were also circumcised with a circumcision not performed by human hands. Your whole self ruled by the flesh was put off when you were circumcised by Christ, having been buried with him in baptism, in which you were also raised with him through your faith in the working of God, who raised him from the dead.

Here we are taught that in water baptism the believer fully identifies with Christ in his death, burial and resurrection, and this equates to a circumcision, a 'circumcision done by

Christ'. It is of course Christ who gives the Holy Spirit, and it is the Spirit who effects the new birth which is confirmed in water baptism. This then is the primary aspect of the circumcision of the heart by the Spirit. It is deep; it is painful for it involves conviction of sin, of wrongdoing and idolatry; the mark of identification with Christ is clear. And then the believer discovers that the circumcising work of the Spirit is ongoing, never finished (in time); a life-long awareness of the deviousness and selfishness of the human heart is the lot of all believers; the only way forward is an ever more intense identity with Christ, and an acceptance of the Spirit's heart surgery, which is always loving, creative, life-saving and good... but sometimes painful too.

Philippians 3:3-4:

> *It is we who are the circumcision [i.e. we who, by the grace of God, have been circumcised in the heart], we who serve God by his Spirit, who boast in Christ Jesus, and who put no confidence in the flesh – though I myself have reasons for such confidence.*

Paul goes on to explain that all that formerly was 'profit' to him (his Jewish credentials, his legalistic righteousness) he now considers but 'loss for the sake of Christ' (v.7). The circumcision of his heart, by the Spirit, has so radically transformed him that his testimony is now:

> *I consider everything a loss because of the surpassing worth of knowing Christ Jesus my Lord, for whose sake I have lost all things. I consider them garbage, that I may gain Christ and be found in him, not having a righteousness of my own that comes from the law, but that which is through faith in Christ – the*

> *righteousness that comes from God on the basis of faith. I want to know Christ – yes, to know the power of his resurrection and participation in his sufferings, becoming like him in his death, and so, somehow, attaining to the resurrection from the dead. (v.8-11)*

Quiet and receptive meditation of this passage is recommended to all who long for a deeper experience of the circumcision of the heart by the Spirit.

Deuteronomy 30:6:

> *The* L{\sc ord} *your God will circumcise your hearts and the hearts of your descendants,* **so that you may love him with all your heart and with all your soul, and live***.*

This magnificent commitment and promise given to the Israelites through Moses in the context of the renewal of the Mosaic covenant, must be so very relevant to the New Covenant and to circumcision by the Spirit, for there can be no higher purpose for the church today, and for each of us within it, but to love the Lord our God with all of our being.

When does heart circumcision take place?

Our comments on the extracts from scripture cited above indicate that we understand them to teach that the primary act of heart circumcision takes place at the new birth, at conversion, subsequently confirmed by water baptism, and that this is followed by a life-long work of the Holy Spirit which deepens, amplifies and intensifies the initial intervention.

The nature, and indeed the necessity or otherwise of the ongoing work of the Spirit, is the subject of differing viewpoints amongst Christians. Is the Spirit's work only gradual, or are there also times, situations and places, when and where, the gradual is greatly accentuated by a particular encounter with God, during which the knife of the Spirit, his fire, his love, his power and his person accomplish a transforming work in the believer's heart?

What then needs to happen after conversion?

It seems probable that most Christians move on in their pilgrimage without giving serious attention to what the Bible says about circumcision of the heart, perhaps because they understand that all the circumcising that was needed was performed in their new birth. Others, occasionally whole communities, whilst appreciating the gracious though, for many, painful work accomplished at their conversion, are deeply exercised by the matter, and, aware of their need, seek God for further circumcising of their heart. They long for a closer walk with Jesus, that Christ be their all in all, that the roots of sin and self be extirpated from their beings, and that they might be sanctified in every part. A longing for purity and holiness is the common characteristic of those who have left us written testimony of how God met with them subsequent to their new birth and further circumcised their heart by the Holy Spirit. Some who have this testimony explain their experience using additional or alternative phrases to 'circumcision of the heart'. Examples are 'second blessing', 'Christian perfection', 'perfect love', 'full salvation' and 'entire salvation'.

Roy and Revel Hession's testimony

In their very special little book *The Calvary Road*,[17] Roy and Revel Hession, a missionary couple, tell of the way God worked firstly in their colleagues, then in them, enabling both to humble themselves, to enter into a deeper experience of brokenness, of cleansing in the blood of Christ and of living in close communion with God.

The couple were working with the Worldwide Evangelization Crusade and had learnt that revival was being experienced on a certain mission field. Roy organised an Easter Conference (April 1947) and invited several workers from this field to come and speak. He writes in the book's preface:

> *As they unfolded their message and gave their testimonies, I discovered that I was the neediest person in the Conference, and was far more in need of being revived than I had ever realized ... As my wife and others humbled themselves before God and experienced the cleansing power of the precious Blood of Jesus, I found myself left high and dry – dry just because I was high. I was humbled by the simplicity of the message, or rather the simplicity of what I had to do to be revived and filled with the Spirit ... it was only afterwards (after the Conference) that I was enabled to give up trying to fit things into my doctrinal scheme and come humbly to the Cross for cleansing from my own personal sins.*[18]

---

17. Roy Hession, *The Calvary Road* (Buckingham, UK: Rickfords Hill Publishing, 2010).
18. Roy Hession, *The Calvary Road*, p.vii.

In the remainder of their book Roy and Revel write of several of the essential elements that had brought them this far, the first being 'brokenness'. It seems clear to us that, subsequent to their conversion, they had been led into a deeper experience of 'the circumcision of the heart by the Spirit'.

John Wesley's teaching

John Wesley's sermon 'The Circumcision of the Heart'[19] was preached at St Mary's Church, Oxford, on 1st January 1733, and no doubt on many other occasions. Readily available on the Internet it is not easy reading for 21st-century man, but well worth the effort nevertheless. Here is an extract:

> *We are convinced, that we are not sufficient of ourselves to help ourselves; that, without the Spirit of God, we can do nothing but add sin to sin; that it is he alone who worketh in us by his mighty power, either to will or to do that which is good; it is impossible for us to think a good thought, without the supernatural assistance of his Spirit, as to create ourselves, or to renew our whole souls in righteousness and true holiness.*[20]

That he believed in a further circumcision subsequent to the initial intervention at new birth is made abundantly clear in Wesley's correspondence. To Joseph Benson he wrote:

> *With all zeal and diligence confirm the brethren (1) in holding fast that whereto they have attained – namely,*

---

19. *Wesley's Standard Sermons, Volume I*, Sermon XIII, pp.263-279.
20. *Wesley's Standard Sermons, Volume I*, Sermon XIII, p.268.

remission of all their sins by faith in the bleeding Lord, and (2) in expecting a second change, whereby they shall be saved from all sin and perfected in love.[21]

And to Sarah Rutter:

Gradual sanctification may increase from the time you are justified, but full deliverance from sin, I believe, is always instantaneous – at least, I never knew an exception.[22]

Was John Wesley correct? Surely the matter is of such great weight that we should not casually set aside the teaching of Wesley and the considerable number of others who have followed his line, with similar consequential experience. Some adjustment for theological or other reasons may be warranted, but Christians today should face up to the clear and vital main thrust of his teaching.

The community at Herrnhut

Many others, individuals and communities, have recorded a major point of transformation in their relationship with God and their fellow believers, which amounted to a profound circumcision of the heart by the Spirit – including conviction of sin, brokenness, repentance, confession, reconciliation with others, renewal in all areas of Christian life, particularly prayer and communion with God. Consider, for example, that mixed group of Christians who, quite early on in the 18th century, began living

---

21. Leonard Ravenhill, *John Wesley*, https://www.sermonindex.net/modules/articles/index.php?view=article&aid=22872 (accessed 21.4.24).
22. Leonard Ravenhill, *John Wesley*, https://www.sermonindex.net/modules/articles/index.php?view=article&aid=22872 (accessed 21.4.24).

together in community, somewhat unhappily, at Herrnhut (meaning The Lord's Watch), in Saxony. They were from various and varied backgrounds, the majority being of the Moravian Church of the Brethren (leader Count Nicholas Zinzendorf); others were Lutheran, Baptist, Catholic or Reformed believers. They held divergent theological and administrative views. Controversy was rife; the situation needed urgent remedial action, and a special Communion service was convened for 13th August 1727.

God prepared the people for participation in the service, and many were convicted of their wrongdoing, un-Christian thinking and sectarian attitudes. During the meeting Zinzendorf prayed, confessing his sins, others followed in the same vein; the Holy Spirit came powerfully upon the assembly. Later the Count wrote:

> *The Saviour permitted to come upon us a Spirit of whom we had hitherto not had any experience or knowledge. Hitherto we had been the leaders and helpers. Now the Holy Spirit himself took full control of everything and everybody.*[23]

Another wrote that the community members had 'been melted together into one';[24] someone else recorded, 'We were baptised by the Holy Spirit himself to one love';[25] it had been, wrote Zinzendorf, 'a day of the outpouring of the Holy Spirit upon the congregation'.[26]

---

23. Oswald J. Smith, *The Moravian Revival* (1727), https://www.heraldofhiscoming.org/index.php/179-past-issues/2008/aug08/2173-the-moravian-revival-1727-8-08 (accessed 30.4.24).
24. Howard A. Snyder, *Signs of the Spirit: How God Reshapes the Church* (Eugene, OR: Wipf & Stock Publishers, 1997), p.133.
25. Ibid.
26. Ibid.

That day, a day of heart circumcision, was truly important for the work the Holy Spirit accomplished then and afterwards. The divine intervention of that day birthed a prayer meeting that would go on for 100 years, and missionary activity that would take the good news of Jesus to many lands.

It has been written that 'it was such a powerful visitation of the Holy Spirit that many referred to it as "a Moravian Pentecost".'[27] And just as the first Christians went out to Judea, Samaria and the ends of the earth, so 'it was not long before men were being sent out from Herrnhut to the West Indies, to North America and to other places nearer home, to carry the Saviour's message of redeeming grace to those who had not heard it'.[28]

We must also note that the children in the Herrnhut community were wonderfully touched by the Spirit, the result being that their supplications had a powerful effect on all around them.

The Holiness movement

This movement's roots are in Puritanism and Pietism, and indeed in the Bible! Its partisans adhere to a first work of grace, that is regeneration or the New Birth, and a subsequent, or second work, also of grace, wherein the Christian is circumcised in the heart by the Spirit and empowered by the same Spirit to live a holy life, a Christ-like life. The Holiness movement greatly influenced the

---

27. Beautiful Feet, *Moravian Revival of 1727*, https://romans1015.com/moravian-revival-2/ (accessed 24.6.24).
28. The Moravian Church, *Moravian History*, http://www.moravian.org.uk/a-historic-church/our-history (accessed 24.6.24).

Moravians, John Wesley and the Methodists, the Salvation Army, many in the Pentecostal movement and in other Christian communities, including the Keswick movement and Faith Mission in the United Kingdom.

Smith Wigglesworth

Born in 1859, not far from Bradford in Yorkshire, into a very poor family, Smith Wigglesworth experienced the riches of God's grace throughout his long life, despite the natural hardships and the spiritual struggles that were his constant lot. Quite late on in adulthood he became an internationally acknowledged evangelist, a man who walked with God, an apostle of faith. But as a child he received no formal education, and, aged six, he was working on a farm in the turnip fields. The family had connections with the local Methodists; his parents were non-practising, but his grandmother was! She was saved, and she took Smith to the Wesleyan Methodist Mission Hall, where, aged eight, the Holy Spirit convicted the boy of sin and drew his attention to Jesus. The congregation, whilst dancing around a coal stove, was singing about the Lamb of God and the blood of Jesus; Smith joined in, and later he said, 'Suddenly I saw that Jesus had died for me . . . I knew that I was born again.'[29] He was born of the Spirit!

A few years later Smith, now 14, was with the Anglicans and was confirmed in the faith, a bishop laying hands on him. For the young adolescent this was not just a ceremony but a dynamic encounter with God the Holy Spirit, and he was filled with an overwhelming joy. Subsequently Smith came

---

29. George Stormont, *Smith Wigglesworth, A Man Who Walked with God* (Tulsa, OK: Harrison House, 1989), p.vi.

to understand that on this occasion the Holy Spirit began a work that was ongoing and culminated in the baptism of the Spirit, which he received some 40 years later.

In 1882 Smith Wigglesworth married Mary Jane Featherstone ('Polly'), a Salvation Army officer. Theirs was a union blessed by God (they had five children), and of the pair it was Polly who, for most of her relatively short life, was particularly equipped and used by the Spirit. She taught her 'Smith' to read. Together they opened a mission hall, and it was she who preached and led, whilst he was in support, particularly in the counselling of enquirers. He put much effort into building his plumbing work into a prosperous business but he fell victim to materialism and to the worst trait of his strong character, his temper, which often got the better of him. Whilst Polly was becoming ever more fervent and consecrated, he was growing colder. This brought about a spiritual crisis in Wigglesworth. In his book *Wigglesworth, A Man Who Walked with God*, George Stormont[30] gives us this account of how the crisis was resolved. Following one argument with Polly, Wigglesworth said to himself:

> 'This won't do in a child of God,' and he determined to meet God at every opportunity. Setting aside ten days, he presented his body a living sacrifice (Rom. 12:1–2). He prayed, wept, soaked in the Word, and pleaded the promises. He faced up to the cross until he began to understand what Paul meant in Galatians 2:20. This is how he described the experience to me: 'God worked the old Wigglesworth-nature out and began

---

30. George Stormont, *Smith Wigglesworth, A Man Who Walked with God* (Tulsa, OK: Harrison House, 1989).

> to work the new Jesus-nature in.' The transformation was obvious to all who knew him. He became the calmest, purest man I ever knew. What he taught after that, he lived ... His sin ... caused him to cry mightily unto God. He reached the place of brokenness. Such brokenness may well be the prerequisite of full spiritual development.[31]

This account tells us that, step by step, the Holy Spirit was doing a circumcising work on Smith Wigglesworth's heart. Then followed a period of great blessing in Bradford, but Smith was hungry for yet more of God, particularly God's power; Acts 1:8 was very present in his mind and heart. He learnt that the Holy Spirit was being poured out abundantly on believers at All Saints Church, Sunderland, with the accompaniment of speaking in tongues as on the day of Pentecost, and subsequent occasions (Acts 2, 8, 10 and 19). Smith went to All Saints, spent some days wrestling with certain convictions he had held until then concerning the Holy Spirit and his workings. His hunger intensified. George Stormont recounts what happened next, as related to him by Wigglesworth:

> I went to the vicarage, and ... said to the vicar's wife, Mrs. Boddy, 'I can rest no longer. I must have these tongues.' ... 'Please lay your hands on me that I may receive tongues.' She rose up and laid her hands on me, and the fire fell. (Just then) she had to go out to answer a knock on the door. It was the best thing that could have happened. I was alone with God. Then He gave me a revelation. Oh, it was wonderful! He

---

31. George Stormont, *Smith Wigglesworth*, p.61.

showed me an empty cross and Jesus glorified. Then I saw that the Lord had purified me. It seemed that God gave me a new vision, and I saw a perfect being within me with mouth open, saying, 'Clean, clean, clean.' When I began to repeat it, I found myself speaking with other tongues. The joy was so great, I could not utter it in my own tongue, and I worshipped God in other tongues as the Spirit gave utterance. It was all as beautiful, as peaceful, as when Jesus said, 'Peace, be still' (Mark 4:39). The tranquillity of that moment and the joy surpassed anything I had ever known. What had I received? I had received the Bible evidence. [32]

He meant evidence of the baptism in the Holy Spirit.

Just a few years later, in 1913, Polly died, and Smith was heart-broken. But she had exhorted him to launch out into an evangelistic ministry of preaching and doing what the first apostles did. He did just that, travelling extensively in the United Kingdom, the United States, Canada, New Zealand, Europe, South Africa and elsewhere until he died in 1947. He preached and ministered in the **power** of the Holy Spirit to large crowds and congregations, and there were many conversions, miracles of healing, acts of deliverance and always a strong emphasis on the importance of **holiness**, humility and compassion in the lives of believers. Stimulating reading regarding this period of Smith Wigglesworth's life and ministry is available on line and in the biographical books by Stanley Frodsham and George Stormont and probably others. He wrote two books, *Ever Increasing Faith* and *Faith That Prevails*, but

---

32. George Stormont, *Smith Wigglesworth*, p.64-65.

primarily he was 'a man of one book', a phrase initially used by John Wesley.

The apostle Paul

In chapter 7 of his letter to the Christians at Rome Paul forcefully describes his struggling with sin and his carnal nature, which he says is his body of death. He seems to shout out aloud, 'What a wretched man I am! Who will rescue me from this body that is subject to death?' (v.24). What are we to understand here? Is Christ's apostle reminiscing on his condition prior to conversion, prior to his Damascus road encounter with Jesus whom he there confessed to be his Lord? Or is Paul openly and honestly describing the present state of his heart? No matter which of these alternatives was motivating Paul's mind whilst he wrote, he knew the remedy for his condition. Verse 25 says it all, 'Thanks be to God, who delivers me through Jesus Christ our Lord!' Paul's heart, it being in the grave condition he described, needed to be circumcised by the Spirit. It seems to us that he must have had an initial heart-circumcising experience at his dramatic first encounter with the risen and ascended Jesus; on that occasion, as a repentant persecutor of Christians, he fell to the ground and humbled himself before his newly found Lord and Saviour. Shortly afterwards, when Ananias prayed for him and the Holy Spirit filled him, the circumcising work of the Spirit was certainly intensified. Very likely there were other occasions when the Spirit worked in Paul in an incisive manner. All this gave the apostle the necessary authority and authenticity to write clearly and convincingly on the subject to the church at Rome (Romans 2:28-29).

Finding Paul in crisis in chapter 7 is initially surprising, even disappointing. How is it that the great man appears to be so distraught; he feels wretched! Could it be that he felt compelled to bare his soul to his readers in order to demonstrate that he and they, in order to know constant purity and holiness, needed certainly more than one, probably more than two circumcision-like interventions on the heart by the Spirit? However, many were the interventions made on his heart; it is clear that Paul was a Spirit-marked man ('I bear on my body the marks of Jesus', Galatians 6:17); he identified with Jesus Christ and him alone ('For to me, to live is Christ', Philippians 1:21); he knew what it meant to be broken ('I have been crucified with Christ and I no longer live, but Christ lives in me', Galatians 2:20).

Paul's challenge to the Galatian Christians

Paul did not forget the Christian communities that he and his 'fellow workers for the kingdom of God' (Colossians 4:11) founded in Europe and Asia Minor. By prayer, return visits, the sending of colleagues to give pastoral ministry (usually short term, for in the early church common practice was to place ongoing Bible ministry and shepherding in the hands of designated local Christians, known as elders); he also wrote letters to the young churches, thereby encouraging, teaching doctrine, holiness, practical and prayerful living and endeavouring to correct errors of belief and behaviour of which he had become aware.

Paul had evidently learnt that the Christians in Galatia were in danger of losing the freedom that they had come to know in Christ, for they, Gentiles, were being negatively influenced by Judaizers (Christian Jews) who believed it necessary for Gentile converts to conform to a number of Old Testament practices, circumcision in particular. So it is that in his letter to them he very plainly, but caringly, restates the teaching that he and, very probably, others had left them with. Here are some of his key points, quoting from J.B. Phillips's translation:

Galatians 3:2-3: 'Did you receive the Spirit of God by trying to keep the Law or by believing the message of the Gospel? Surely you can't be so idiotic as to think that a man begins his spiritual life in the Spirit and then completes it by reverting to outward observances?'

3:14: 'God's purpose is therefore plain: that the blessing promised to Abraham [justification by faith alone] might reach the Gentiles through Jesus Christ, and the Spirit might become available to us all by faith.'

3:26: 'For now that you have faith in Christ you are all sons of God.'

4:6-7: 'It is because you really are his sons that God has sent the Spirit of his Son into your hearts to cry "Father, dear Father".'

5:1-2: 'Plant your feet firmly therefore within the freedom that Christ has won for us, and do not let yourselves be caught again in the shackles of slavery. Listen! I, Paul, say this to you as solemnly as I can: if you consent to be circumcised then Christ will be of no use to you at all.'

5:6-7: 'In Jesus Christ there is no validity in either circumcision or uncircumcision; it is a matter of faith, faith which expresses itself in love. You were making splendid progress; who put you off the course you had set for the truth?'

5:16: 'Here is my advice. Live your whole life in the Spirit and you will not satisfy the desires of your lower nature.'

5:17-23: Paul next sets out the contrast between the 'activities of the lower nature' and the magnificent 'fruit' that the 'Spirit produces in human life'.

5:24-26: Paul explains what Christians need to do in order that the Spirit might produce his fruit in them. 'Those who belong to Christ have crucified their old nature with all that it loved and lusted for. If our lives are centred in the Spirit, let us be guided by the Spirit. Let us not be ambitious for our own reputations, for that only means making each other jealous.'

6:12-16: Paul recapitulates and states what really counts. 'These men are always urging you to be circumcised – what are they after? . . . They want you to be circumcised so that they may be able to boast about your submission to their ruling. Yet God forbid that I should boast about anything or anybody except the cross of our Lord Jesus Christ, which means that the world is a dead thing to me and I am a dead man to the world. But in Christ it is not circumcision or uncircumcision that counts but the power of new birth. To all who live by this principle, to the true Israel of God, may there be peace and mercy!'

Earlier we have noted that in the letter to the church at Rome Paul employs the phrase 'circumcision of the heart by the Spirit'. In his correspondence to the Galatians the phraseology is different (Galatians 6:15 NIV, 'what counts is the new creation') but, or so it would seem to us, the meaning is identical to that in Romans 2:28-29. Paul's earnest purpose was to appeal to the Galatian Christians to say 'no' to physical circumcision, and 'yes' to the work of the Holy Spirit, i.e. the circumcision of the heart, which necessitates wholehearted identity with Christ crucified for them.

Today there are legalistic voices within Christian churches and associations, and most Christians would probably be willing to confess to guilt in this area; perhaps we have been over zealous regarding doctrines not essential to the salvation message, or, more importantly, we have pushed to the fore dogmas and practices, the bases for which are outside scripture. On a much happier note it is good to acknowledge that today Jesus has a mighty army of Spirit-circumcised 'hearts' who seek to avoid legalism in their relationships, place their emphasis on the communication of the gospel and say to their Lord, 'Here am I. Send me!'

Divine cardiology

Recently my wife and I listened to an address during which the teacher spoke of his own cardiac condition in order to illustrate his subject. Breathlessness and tiredness had incited him to seek medical advice. He had undergone a quite painful examination that had shown a heart valve to be defective. He is now on appropriate medication, and shortly a surgeon will insert a stent in an artery which should improve his situation. He is in the capable hands of specialists who know the human heart. Other treatment may follow.

David, the psalmist-shepherd-king, knew that his moral-spiritual heart was not in good health, and he also knew that his God was the only 'consultant' able to put things right. In Psalm 139:23-24 David writes, 'Search me, God, and know my heart; test me and know my anxious thoughts. See if there is any offensive way in me, and lead me in the way everlasting.'

David was willing to be searched out and tested, which would undoubtedly occasion him moral pain and conviction of wrongdoing and unfaithfulness, but he longed for God to cleanse him, purify his thoughts and, surely, we must say it, circumcise his heart. With the words we read in Psalm 51:10-11 he prayed with all his soul, 'Create in me a pure heart, O God, and renew a steadfast spirit within me. Do not cast me from your presence or take your Holy Spirit from me.' He is a broken man who knows that his deliverance is in God alone: 'My sacrifice, O God, is a broken spirit; a broken and contrite heart you, God, will not despise' (v.17).

An Old Testament parallel

In the sixth chapter of the book which bears his name, Isaiah describes the awesome face-to-face encounter he had with the Lord Almighty. The imagery is not the same, but what God did to and for the prophet has much similarity with what God accomplishes when he circumcises a heart by the Spirit. In circumcision the Spirit is a knife or scalpel, which cuts into the heart in order to cleanse it of sin and guilt, make it holy and to mark it with a new identity (that of a Jew, inwardly). In Isaiah's case the instrument is a live coal taken from the altar, with which the lips are touched in order to take away guilt, atone for sin, render them (the lips) clean, and convey a commission (to go and tell this people . . .). Merging the two sets of imagery helps us to understand the work the Holy Spirit accomplished in the company at Herrnhut, which gave birth to extensive propagation of the gospel.

All the aforementioned persons and communities knew the wondrous sanctifying power of the Spirit; they knew 'righteousness, peace and joy in the Holy Spirit' (Romans 14:17), together with the hardship and suffering which were occasioned by their testimony. Paul was, therefore, led to pray for the Roman community, 'May the God of hope fill you with all joy and peace as you trust in him, so that you may overflow with hope by the power of the Holy Spirit' (Romans 15:13). Paul's motivation for what he wrote to the Romans was 'that the Gentiles [i.e. his initial readers and most of us] might become an offering acceptable to God, sanctified by the Holy Spirit' (Romans 15:16). Both 2 Thessalonians 2:13 and 1 Peter 1:2 speak of 'the sanctifying work of the Spirit'. This mighty work is indispensable in the life of a Christian.

Another text, 1 Corinthians 6:11, tells us that Jesus and the Holy Spirit together wash, justify and sanctify those who come to God for salvation and transformation. 'You were washed, you were sanctified, you were justified in the name of the Lord Jesus Christ and by the Spirit of our God.' We understand sanctification to mean *separation from* and *setting apart to*.

It is therefore the condition of the heart that determines whether or not a person is a Christian.

See also Deuteronomy 6:5; 10:16; 30:6 and Jeremiah 4:4; 24:7.

8
Calls to Service and Ministry

Jack London's 1903 novel *The Call of the Wild* is set in the Yukon at the time of the Klondike Gold Rush. Its hero is a dog named Buck, a large and strong cross between a Saint Bernard and a Scottish Collie. Brought up in the security of a good home in California, Buck is kidnapped, ill-treated and sold into the only-the-fittest-survive society of the Yukon. He has a succession of cruel and selfish masters and many brutal adventures. However, his last master was different, kind and understanding; Buck was devoted to him. But the dog, a leader amongst his kind, was drawn ever-more irresistibly to the largely untouched-by-man natural world around him; he was gripped by 'the call of the wild'. After the death of his beloved master Buck took his place in the world where he really belonged, becoming the leader of a pack of wolves. 'The call' had got the better of him, and in the wild he found satisfaction and fulfilment.

We must ask ourselves, 'Has Jesus' call, winged home into our hearts by the Holy Spirit, got the better of us?' To whom do we really belong? Where does our Master want us to be, what does he want us to be, and to be doing?

Here we must emphasise that the call we should have in view is not primarily for that minority of Christians whom the Spirit calls into some form of what we often describe as 'full-time Christian service'. Rather it is the call that the Spirit addresses to all the 'new-born', all in the body of Christ, each and every member of the 'royal priesthood of all believers'. For all of us it is a call to discipleship; we remember Jesus' call to Simon and the others, 'Come, follow me!' It is also a call to service: 'Go, and make disciples!'

Happily, the experience of being called is commonplace for everyone; it happens all the time. Mother opens the outside door of the home and calls out to her children, 'Come in, dinner's ready!' We might find ourselves in an unpleasant situation when we must cry out to an owner, 'Call off your dogs!' Sometime in the past we may have received our 'Call-up papers'. We may have had a narrow escape, and describe it to friends as 'A close call!' The anticipated results of an election may be 'Too close to call'. Should we find ourselves in a Court of Law we will be 'Called upon to tell the truth, and . . .' Rather more pleasant is hearing the referee say, before the match starts, 'Your call, heads or tails?'

Is it not wonderfully encouraging to be called by God? To have a divine calling, a God-given vocation? However, prior to receiving a call to service, we must first have responded to the Saviour's call to us as sinners to come to him for his gift of salvation. In 1883 Fanny J. Crosby wrote these lines, which have subsequently spoken graciously to many needy hearts:

> *Jesus is tenderly calling you home.*
> *Calling today, calling today;*
> *Why from the sunshine of love will you roam,*
> *Further and further away?*
>
> *Calling today, calling today,*
> *Jesus is calling, is tenderly calling today.*[33]

How wonderful it is to be called in this way! The apostle Jude addressed a letter 'To those who have been called, who are loved by God the Father and kept by Jesus Christ'.

Within the Saviour's call to come to him for pardon and salvation, and our recognition of Jesus' Lordship, there is also an inherent call to service. Paul wrote to Timothy concerning God, who 'has saved us and **called** us to a holy life' (2 Timothy 1:9). The call to holiness is an essential element in being born again, and it includes a call to service.

A selection from the multitude who have responded to the Spirit's call

Abraham

'By faith Abraham, when **called** to go to a place he would later receive as his inheritance, obeyed and went, even though he did not know where he was going' (Hebrews 11:8). He upped sticks and moved from Mesopotamia to Canaan, the promised land. Abraham was to experience many twists and turns in the fulfilment of God's plan for him and the people, but through the years of trial and testing the call he had received remained clear in his heart,

---

33. Fanny Crosby (1820–1915), 'Jesus is Calling', https://hymnary.org/text/jesus_is_tenderly_calling_you_home (accessed 28.3.24).

and in most of his actions. His was a call that had vital relevance for the whole world, for his generation and every succeeding generation till the end of time. In response to his obedience to the call, and his faith, God made covenant promises to him. Surely God the Holy Spirit was in all of that, and he is still wonderfully overseeing the fulfilment of the promises.

Isaiah 51:2 is a very helpful comment on Abraham's call and an important practical aspect of how it was outworked; God speaking, 'Look to Abraham, your father, and to Sarah, who gave you birth. When I **called** him he was only one man, and I blessed him and made him many.' Maybe you too were alone when the Lord called you; it could be that you will need the help of one or more persons in the outworking/fulfilment of the call.

Moses

Having fled Egypt, leaving behind his cruelly oppressed compatriots, Moses found refuge and a wife in Midian. Whilst he was tending his father-in-law's flock the Lord appeared to him in flames of fire within a bush (see Exodus 3). 'God called to him from within the bush, "Moses! Moses!" And Moses said, "Here I am."' The call he received was to bring the Israelites out of Egypt into the promised land. Moses' call, just like Abraham's, involved major participation in redemption's unfolding story. For Moses, too, the Holy Spirit was most certainly in the call.

To us it seems reasonable to consider the calls to Abraham and Moses as exceptional and extraordinary. But their God is our God and we should assume that he, as the Lord of all whom he calls to participation in the propagation of the gospel, the setting free of captives and the bringing in of Jesus' reign, rightly assesses the value and importance of every individual and collective response. A great multitude of redeemed and chosen persons have heard the Lord's call, and have said, 'Here I am,' and undertaken their part in the building of Christ's church. All will receive the commendation, 'Well done, good and faithful servant! You have been faithful with a few things; I will put you in charge of many things. Come and share your master's happiness!' (Matthew 25:23). May this encourage those whose 'call' is known to few, who work out the 'call' secretly, often in the shadows of our world.

Bezalel and Oholiab

These two highly skilled craftsmen were chosen and appointed (called) to lead the team that would construct and furnish the Tent of Meeting (the Tabernacle). The work to be done was practical with eternally important spiritual overtones; excellence in skill, attitude and relationships were essential.

This was the charge that the Lord addressed to Moses:

> *See I have chosen Bezalel son of Uri, the son of Hur, of the tribe of Judah, and I have filled him with the Spirit of God, with wisdom, with understanding, with knowledge and with all kinds of skills – to make artistic designs for work in gold, silver and bronze, to cut and set stones, to work in wood, and to engage in all kinds of crafts. Moreover, I have appointed Oholiab son of Ahisamak, of the tribe of Dan, to help him. Also I*

have given ability to all the skilled workers to make everything I have commanded you: the tent of meeting, the ark of the covenant law with the atonement cover on it, and all the other furnishings of the tent – the table and its articles, the pure gold lampstand and all its accessories, the altar of incense, the altar of burnt offering and all its utensils, the basin with its stand – and also the woven garments, both the sacred garments for Aaron the priest and the garments for his sons when they serve as priests, and the anointing oil and fragrant incense for the Holy Place. They are to make them just as I commanded you. (Exodus 31:2-11)

What a task! Who today possesses the skills necessary to face up to such a wide-ranging and demanding job description? No doubt the two lead men had benefited from a thorough and disciplined apprenticeship; they were workmen who had no need to be ashamed! But, in addition, Bezalel was filled with the Holy Spirit; Oholiab too very probably. They were godly men.

The Scriptures teach a high standard work ethic; these two had learnt to aspire after excellence, and the Spirit of God filled them. Moses had learnt to shepherd flocks of sheep, and this led him to an encounter with the living God from whom he received a call. Saul of Tarsus learnt tent making, and he was also a diligent student of Judaism. These acquired skills were vital preparatory factors in the calls to service and ministry they each received later in life.

The account in Acts 6 of seven men being called to carry out practical service in the Jerusalem community tells us that they were all filled with the Spirit. They had learnt ordinary life skills, attained high standards, been filled with the Spirit and were ready for a call-up.

In these and other biblical accounts, and also in the lives of Christians we read of, or know, there are principles concerning learning, career choices, and being filled with the Holy Spirit that we, particularly young Christians, need to be aware of. Young people considering Bible school or some form of theological training with a view to subsequent full- or part-time engagement in Christian ministry, would do well to take into account the relevance to them of the examples set by those who accepted that God's plan for them was that they first learn a skill that would enable them to earn daily bread for their dependants and themselves, and furthermore afford them workplace experience. A young Christian will normally gain biblical knowledge and discipleship training during the work-learning period. Thereafter, on the solid foundation acquired, some form of further biblical education and/or ministry training can be envisaged. Throughout, the Christian's ear will be attuned to the call of the Spirit which may reach him progressively or suddenly.

Joshua, Barnabas and Saul

The Lord called Joshua to be Moses' successor, but he did not communicate the call directly to the man he chose; God called Joshua via Moses. 'The LORD said to Moses, "Take Joshua son of Nun, a man in whom is the spirit, and lay your hand on him' (Numbers 27:18 NIV 1984).[34] Verse

---

34. Alternative rendering, https://www.biblegateway.com/passage/?search=Numbers+27%3A18&version=NIVUK (accessed 28.3.24).

23 confirms that Moses did as he was commanded; thus Joshua, having been called, was now commissioned.

Similarly, the 'call' that Barnabas and Saul received to set out on a missionary journey (Acts 13:1-3) was delivered to them by the Holy Spirit when they were in community with other prophets and teachers. The Spirit said to all, '"Set apart for me Barnabas and Saul for the work to which I have called them." So after they had fasted and prayed, they placed their hands on them and sent them off.' We note that the laying on of hands is often associated with the work of the Holy Spirit and the implementation of callings. Are we, and the communities to which we belong, awake to the calls that the Spirit speaks and reveals amongst us, and thereafter willing and eager to set apart and send off the called-out persons, so doing by means of the laying on of hands?

The boy Samuel and Timothy

The third chapter of 1 Samuel relates the story of the night when the Lord called Samuel three times by name, and then a fourth time when, acting on Eli's advice, the youngster responded, saying to the Lord, 'Speak, for your servant is listening.' Samuel then had to listen to a revelation of judgment that was soon to fall on Eli and his family; this must have been harsh listening for the boy, and he certainly did not enjoy having to share it with Eli when morning dawned. Samuel had received a divine call to the ministry of prophet.

Some are young, even very young, when the Spirit calls them to service, e.g. the child prophets amongst the persecuted Huguenots. Are we alive to such possibilities today?

It was early in Paul's second missionary journey when he and his companions met a young believer named Timothy at Lystra (Acts 16:1-5). The youngster, probably then in his teens, joined the travelling team and entered on a long association with Paul. Through Paul, and no doubt others, Timothy grew in discipleship and became one of the apostle's trusted assistants, delegating to him considerable pioneering, church-planting and pastoral responsibilities. His calling was confirmed throughout the course he was led to follow, and also, on at least one occasion, when the elders (the pastoral team in a local church) laid their hands on him, and he received a spiritual gift through a prophetic message (1 Timothy 4:14).

Isaiah

Isaiah's graphic and awe-inspiring account (in chapter 6 of his book) of his encounter with the Lord and his seraphs, tells how he saw God (presumably in a vision) in his holiness and glory, how he (Isaiah) was smitten with an overwhelming sense of sin and guilt, how his guilt was taken away and his sin atoned for, and how the voice of the Lord called him to service, 'Saying, "Whom shall I send? And who will go for us?"' Isaiah's reply was. 'Here am I. Send me!' Then the Lord commissioned his servant saying, 'Go, and tell this people.'

The Holy Spirit has used this account to speak to and call to service a great multitude of witnesses to Jesus, the resurrection and the life, from the day of his ascension followed by the day of Pentecost, to now.

'You will receive power when the Holy Spirit comes on you; and you will be my witnesses in Jerusalem, and in Judea and Samaria, and to the ends of the earth' (Acts 1:8). In other words, 'Go tell this people.'

Saul of Tarsus

Saul's encounter with Jesus, the risen Lord, which occurred when he was bent on doing all he could to obliterate all testimony to the Christ, and the events that followed shortly afterwards, are clearly documented in the Book of Acts. Chapter 9 records the events, and in chapters 22 and 26 we find the records of the accounts Saul/Paul later gave to, firstly, the crowd at Jerusalem and later to King Agrippa at Caesarea (maybe others such as Festus were present). Grouping the information given in the three passages we note that a call to service was embodied in Jesus' call to Saul to acknowledge him as Lord. This Saul did, and his subsequent writings confirm that this was his conversion experience. Now born again, having a new Lord and Master but blinded by the brilliance of what he had seen, Saul was led on and greatly helped by his newly discovered brethren.

One of these was Ananias, a stalwart disciple of Jesus, who received a specific call from the Lord to go to Saul and to minister to him. He laid his hands on Saul who was healed of his blindness and filled with the Holy Spirit. Ananias then delivered the message the Lord had entrusted to him:

> *The God of our ancestors has chosen you to know his will and to see the Righteous One and to hear words*

> *from his mouth. You will be his witness to all people of what you have seen and heard. (22:14)*

Ananias then urged Saul to be baptised in water, and he was.

As the apostle to the Gentiles Saul/Paul spent the remainder of his time on earth working out the call to service and ministry he had received over a very short period of just a few days. Here we should add that there were further occasions when he received particular calls from the Spirit; see, for example, Acts 16:6-10 where we are told that Paul and his companions were 'kept by the Holy Spirit from preaching the word' in certain places, because a new and unimagined 'call' was about to be given to them.

> *During the night Paul had a vision of a man of Macedonia standing and begging him, 'Come over to Macedonia and help us.' After Paul had seen the vision, we got ready at once to leave for Macedonia, concluding that God had **called** us to preach the gospel to them. (Acts 16:9-10)*

Since the days of Paul and his friends a great many Christians have similarly received the Spirit's call, conveyed to them over a brief period with breath-taking clarity and life-transforming power. Nevertheless, for many Christians sensitivity to and understanding of the Spirit's call grows over a longer time span and involves a number of factors, e.g. attentive reading of scripture, encounters with representatives of groups of needy persons (from neighbourhoods, villages or countries with little or no Christian presence), becoming aware of particular social needs, learning about places where Christians are persecuted, and lots more sign-posts which the Spirit uses to show us what the nature of God's call to us is.

David Brainerd (1718–1747)

Born into a large Connecticut family David Brainerd's life was short, but many have found inspiration and encouragement in reading accounts of his brief pilgrimage. The many include Christians who, feeling convinced of the nature of God's plan for them, embarked on specific preparation for service, then, for diverse reasons, were stopped in their tracks, led to humbly seek fresh guidance from the Lord, which, often following deep repentance, they received and then moved on, hand-in-hand with the Master in their true calling. So it was for David Brainerd.

Whilst in his early twenties he had a conversion experience, and very soon afterwards entered Yale with the intent of being prepared for ordained ministry. Shortly afterwards his health deteriorated, and he spent some months in convalescence. He returned to Yale and soon found himself in hot water for speaking unwisely and ungraciously of one of his tutors; he was expelled. He apologised later but the damage to his ecclesiastical aspirations had been done, and the road he hoped would lead to ordination turned into a cul-de-sac. John Piper has written, 'Brainerd felt cut off from his calling.'[35]

But God had a different and life-changing call in reserve for the young man. The Holy Spirit would lead him into areas he had not imagined, or so it would seem!

---

35. John Piper, 'David Brainerd', https://www.desiringgod.org/books/david-brainerd (accessed 28.3.24).

Brainerd became a man of prayer, and was guided by the Holy Spirit, mostly via discerning evangelical leaders such as Jonathan Dickinson and Jonathan Edwards, to engage in working amongst the native American Indians, who, for the most part, were unwelcoming of white settlers. On his first journey to the Delaware Indians, Brainerd camped just outside their settlement, intending to visit them the next day. Unknown to him he was being closely followed by a group of warriors whose task was to kill him. What happened was later recounted by F.W. Boreham.

> *When the braves drew closer to Brainerd's tent they saw the paleface on his knees. And as he prayed, suddenly a rattlesnake slipped to his side, lifted up its head, flicked its forked tongue almost in his face, and then, without any apparent reason, glided swiftly away into the brushwood. 'The Great Spirit is with the paleface!' the Indians said; and they accorded him a prophet's welcome.*

Brainerd's diary gives clear confirmation that he had been called 'to pray much'.[36]

His fruitful ministry amongst Indian tribes spanned just three years, but the impact of his calling and his life have reverberated ever since in the hearts of many. Tuberculosis forced him to stop working; through his last months he was cared for in Jonathan Edward's home, his nurse being Jonathan's daughter Jerusha. She too contracted the disease and died of it some four months after David.

---

36. Fred Barlow, 'David Brainerd: Missionary', https://www.wholesomewords.org/missions/biobrain.html (accessed 28.3.24).

Charles Thomas Studd (1860–1931)

In wholehearted response to God's call Charles Studd spent fruitful years as a missionary in China and then India. In his earlier years he had experienced success in sport (notably as a very good cricketer), and as a student. Still a schoolboy, he accepted Christ as his Saviour and Master. Whilst in China he married Priscilla Stewart, also a missionary, and together they were to know hardship and privation, but also great joy in serving their Lord.

The couple returned to England in 1906, and not long after Studd became increasingly concerned about the need for pioneer missionary endeavour in Central Africa, but there were obstacles to his going out to that area – medical advice was unfavourable and financial support had been withdrawn. In spite of these factors Studd said to the Missionary Committee, 'Gentlemen, God has called me to go, and I will go. I will blaze a trail, though my grave may only become a stepping stone that younger men may follow.'[37] He went, sailing to Africa in 1910 and dying there in 1931. He was called by the Spirit and just before his death wrote, 'My only joys ... are that when God has given me a work to do, I have not refused it.'[38] His wife did not see him for many years, and she too sacrificed much for the advance of the Kingdom in Africa.

Charles Studd founded the Worldwide Evangelisation Crusade (WEC), now known as Worldwide Evangelisation for Christ.

---

37. Stephen Ross, 'C.T. Studd: Cricketer and Pioneer', https://www.wholesomewords.org/children/biocc/biostuddcc.html (accessed 28.3.24).
38. Stephen Ross, 'C.T. Studd: Cricketer and Pioneer', https://www.wholesomewords.org/children/biocc/biostuddcc.html (accessed 28.3.24).

Andrew van der Bijl

Andrew van der Bijl, better known as Brother Andrew or 'God's Smuggler', was born into a poor Dutch family in 1928. He sought and found adventure in the Dutch Army, was badly wounded serving in Indonesia and hospitalised. The cheerful and Christ-centred caring of the Franciscan nurses made a profound impression on him and he began to read the Bible given to him by his mother. The Holy Spirit enlightened him, and lying there on his sick bed he came to Jesus, asking for forgiveness and accepting the salvation that the Saviour had obtained for him by his propitiatory death on the cross.

God led Andrew on, rapidly it would seem, and he went to Glasgow to study and train at the WEC Missionary Training College. It was the 1950s and the iron curtain was in place. Andrew became acquainted with the situation of Christians and their communities in communist countries; lack of liberty, oppression and persecution were rife. Andrew van der Bijl heard the call of the Spirit to act on behalf of his persecuted brethren. In particular, it is said, the Holy Spirit spoke to him through Revelations 3:2, 'Wake up! Strengthen what remains and is about to die.' Andrew took this as a call to him to go to the oppressed Christians, bringing to them practical help (including supplies of Bibles which they sorely lacked), encouragement and ministry.

He was joined by others; the mission Open Doors was formed, and today this organisation takes succour to persecuted Christians in many countries and in various political and religious circumstances.

A challenging quote:

> *We have heard the Macedonian call today,*
> *Send the light! Send the light!*
> *And a golden off'ring at the cross we lay,*
> *Send the light! Send the light!*
>
> C.H. Gabriel[39]

---

39. C.H. Gabriel (1890), 'Send the Light', https://hymnary.org/text/theres_a_call_comes_ringing_oer_the_rest (accessed 28.3.24).

9

Leading and Guiding

At around 3.45 pm on 16th February 1909 a powerful deflagration occurred in a gallery situated some 250 meters below the surface at West Stanley Colliery, County Durham, England. The explosion was caused by firedamp (a mixture of methane gas and air) spread by coal dust; 168 men and boys died, either in or as a result of the blast. It was a disaster and a tragedy, but there were survivors. These included a group of 27 who found a pocket where the air was relatively clean. Whilst waiting in the darkness one of them began to hum a hymn tune, and moments later all joined in with the words:

> Lead, kindly Light, amidst the gloom of evening.
> Lord, lead me on . . .
> The night is dark, and I am far from home,
> Direct my feet; I do not ask to see
> The distant scene; one step enough for me.[40]

---

40. John Henry Newman (1833), 'Lead, kindly Light, amid the encircling gloom', https://hymnary.org/text/lead_kindly_light_amid_the_encircling_gl (accessed 29.3.24).

When John Henry Newman wrote these lines in 1833 he was convalescing from illness and poignantly and humbly expressed his need to his heavenly Father, but he could hardly have imagined that years later a group of entombed miners would use his words as a prayer for divine leading from their dire situation.

The Bible attests that God leads and guides; he has done this, and continues to do so, for his people Israel, for humanity as a whole, for the church and each and every one of us personally. Sometimes the divine leading is very evident, visual and dramatic, as, for instance, during the early months of Israel's exodus from Egypt: 'By day the Lord went ahead of them in a pillar of cloud to guide them on their way and by night in a pillar of fire to give them light, so that they could travel by day or night' (Exodus 13:21). At other times God's guiding is much less evident, for it is by the quiet, often hidden supervision of events that he chooses to lead his children on. This is illustrated beautifully in the story of Isaac and Rebekah (see Genesis 24). Certainly, the Lord God never tires, never falters in this or any other aspect of his being and doing. 'He tends his flock like a shepherd: he gathers the lambs in his arms and carries them close to his heart; he gently leads those that have young' (Isaiah 40:11). Leading and guiding is an integral part of the Good Shepherd's role, and that of the Holy Spirit too.

God the Father leads and guides us because he is paternal. All fathers who love and care endeavour to give the appropriate level of leading and guidance to their children, taking into account their age, degree of maturity, personality and intellectual, moral and spiritual capacities. Divine leading and guidance are much in evidence throughout scripture. God is a Shepherd, Israel's Shepherd (Psalm 80), also a personal Shepherd (Psalm 23) and he has always led his people on. God is the Lord of Hosts, or Armies, who leads his people on in the battle against the powers of darkness. In 1903 George A. Young, a rural and far from rich preacher in America, wrote these lines (see Isaiah 43:2), which are probably largely autobiographical, for he had suffered hardship, privation and opposition; his adversaries had burnt down the house he had valiantly built for his family:

In shady, green pastures, so rich and so sweet,
God leads his dear children along;
Where the water's cool flow bathes the weary one's feet,
God leads his dear children along.
Some through the waters, some through the flood,
Some through the fire, but all through the blood;
Some through great sorrow, but God gives a song,
In the night season and all the day long.[41]

In 1821 James Edmeston wrote this hymn, a prayer, for the children of the London Orphan Asylum:

Lead us, heavenly Father, lead us
O'er the world's tempestuous sea;
Guard us, guide us, keep us, feed us,
For we have no help but thee;
Yet possessing every blessing,
If our God our Father be.[42]

---

41. George A. Young (1903), 'In shady, green pastures, so rich and so sweet', https://hymnary.org/text/in_shady_green_pastures_so_rich_and_so (accessed 29.3.24).
42. James Edmeston (1821), 'Lead us heavenly Father, lead us o'er the world's tempestuous sea', https://hymnary.org/text/lead_us_heavenly_father_lead_us_oer (accessed 29.3.24).

Almost a century earlier, in 1736, Philip Doddridge penned these lines which have subsequently strengthened many footsore pilgrims:

O God of Bethel, by whose hand thy people still are fed,
Who through this weary pilgrimage
Hast all our fathers led.[43]

Readers probably recall the story of Jacob's meeting with God at Bethel (see Genesis 28).

His father, Isaac, had sent him off to the East with the intent that he finds there a wife; quite a daunting mission. He needed guidance and leading from God. One night, when he was not far from Haren and sleeping with a stone for pillow, he had a dream. He saw a ladder set up on the earth, the top of it reaching to heaven. The angels of God were ascending and descending on the ladder, and the Lord, Yahweh, stood above it. He said:

I am the LORD, the God of your father Abraham and the God of Isaac. I will give you and your descendants the land on which you are lying. Your descendants will be like the dust of the earth, and you will spread out to the west and to the east, to the north and to the south. All peoples on earth will be blessed through you and your offspring. I am with you and will watch over you wherever you go, and I will bring you back to this land. I will not leave you until I have done what I have promised you. (Genesis 28:13-15)

---

43. Philip Doddridge (1736), 'O God of Bethel, by whose hand', https://hymnary.org/text/o_god_of_bethel_by_whose_hand (accessed 29.3.24).

Jacob awoke and said, 'Surely the LORD is in this place, and I was not aware of it' (v.16). He was afraid and said, 'How awesome is this place! This is none other than the house of God; this is the gate of heaven' (v.17). The story continues with Jacob's act of consecration, his vow to God, his meeting with Rachel and much else which illustrate the vagaries and testing of pilgrim living. We can learn a lot about divine leading and guidance from Jacob's story; it tells us that our Father has a plan for us, that he awaits obedience on our part, desires the very best for us, that he is sovereign in all things, that he has his own inimitable ways of making known his plan to his children; he is the God of Bethel, by whose hand his people still are led and fed.

God the Son, Jesus the Good Shepherd, the Teacher, the disciples' Master, the apostle and high priest whom we confess leads and guides in so many ways, and always in a manner appropriate to the person or people concerned. He leads us to the open spaces to teach us, to the storm-torn lake to behold his power, to the desert to learn how to overcome Satan and his agents, to the mountain to see him as he really is, to Calvary to be broken in spirit and discover union with him in his suffering, to the mount of commissioning and to the upper room to be endued with power from on high.

Whether it be his flock or his army Jesus always leads from the front. His voice is clear and comforting, but also commanding. With gladness his disciples hear what he says, and they follow him to green pastures, to the valley of the shadow of death, to the field of spiritual combat.

Fanny J. Crosby wrote many songs with which Christians today wholeheartedly identify; this is one:

> *All the way my Saviour leads me—*
> *What have I to ask beside?*
> *Can I doubt his tender mercy,*
> *Who through life has been my guide?*[44]

Because she was blind Fanny's testimony carries added conviction. We are also indebted to her for these words:

> *All the way my Saviour leads me—*
> *Oh, the fullness of his love!*
> *Perfect love to me is promised*
> *In my Father's house above.*
> *When my spirit, clothed immortal,*
> *Wings its flight to realms of day,*
> *This my song through endless ages:*
> *Jesus led me all the way.*[45]

'He led them by a straight way to a city where they could settle' (Psalm 107:7). For Christians the city is out of this world!

Readers who, at this point, desire to make or renew a commitment to Jesus, he who leads and guides, may find these lines written by W.C. Martin helpful:

> *Where he may lead me, I will go,*
> *For I have learned to trust him so,*

---

44. Fanny Crosby (1875), 'All the way my Saviour leads me', https://hymnary.org/text/all_the_way_my_savior_leads_me (accessed 29.3.24).
45. Fanny Crosby (1875), 'All the way my Saviour leads me', https://hymnary.org/text/all_the_way_my_savior_leads_me (accessed 29.3.24).

And I remember 'twas for me,
That he was slain on Calvary

Jesus shall lead me night and day,
Jesus shall lead me all the way;
He is the truest Friend to me,
For I remember Calvary.[46]

Being led or guided by the Holy Spirit

In Old Testament times the Holy Spirit led, directed and inspired God's servants, prophets, priests, kings and all the people, usually when they were obedient and submissive, but also when they were not; the 40 years of wandering (turning in circles) in the Sinai Desert are testimony to this. Centuries later King David reigned; he was not always in tune with God's leading, but in one of his penitential psalms in our Bibles, he humbly prays, 'Teach me to do your will, for you are my God; may your good Spirit lead me on level ground' (Psalm 143:10). He was to learn that the Holy Spirit wanted to lead and guide whatever the nature of the terrain he was on; he was to know uphill struggles against enemies, miry marshes where those nearest to him were treacherous and sweet pastures where peace and harmony were everywhere present in his kingdom.

In the context of the Mosaic Covenant one of the means God used for leading the people was to speak to them through the Levite priests by means of the Urim and Thummim. This is explained in Exodus 28:30 and referred to elsewhere, for example Ezra 2:63. It would seem that

---

46. C.M. Martin (1864–1914), 'Where He may lead me I will go', https://hymnary.org/text/where_he_may_lead_me_i_will_go (accessed 29.3.24).

they were oracles through whom the priests could put to the Lord their enquiries, or those of other persons, but little seems to be known regarding their functioning. We mention the matter because we assume that when God spoke by this means it was the Holy Spirit who was at work.

Throughout the Old Testament dispensation, the guiding anointing of the Spirit came upon many, and this was particularly so in the closing phase of the era, regarding John the Baptist, who from birth was filled with the Holy Spirit and was led during his short period of ministry to do and say many Spirit-inspired things. Then Jesus came to bring the Old Testament era to conclusion and usher in the New; he benefitted constantly from the leading of the Spirit. In Luke 4 we learn that 'Jesus, full of the Holy Spirit, left the Jordan and was led by the Spirit into the wilderness, where for forty days he was tempted by the devil' (4:1-2). Oh, how amazing is the leading of the Spirit; he led our Lord to a place of severe temptation and testing. That must help us to accept, maybe understand, some of the leadings of the Spirit that we and the worldwide church, especially persecuted believers, experience today. Shortly after leaving the desert 'Jesus returned to Galilee in the power of the Spirit ... he was teaching ... and everyone praised him' (4:14-15). Yes, the Holy Spirit does lead into ways of pleasantness ... but not always! To this reality the lives of John the Baptist, Jesus and the disciples give clear and eloquent testimony.

On the day of Pentecost Simon Peter became a Spirit-led preacher; he was led to speak on Joel chapter 2 in order to explain to the crowd the mighty outpouring of the Holy Spirit that they had in some measure witnessed. He was led to declare, 'This is what was spoken by the prophet Joel!'

This wonderful leading of the Spirit was of inestimable importance to the disciples and their hearers on that day, and will remain so for the church and the world until the end of time. The story related in The Acts of the Apostles could more accurately be entitled The Acts of the Holy Spirit, the Acts including deeds, signs and wonders, saving and regenerating works and leading. The strong impression made on us when reading the Book of Acts is that the Holy Spirit was leading all the way, second by second, irrespective of whether he is mentioned. Here are the occasions when the Spirit and his leading are specifically mentioned:

Acts 8:29: 'The Spirit told Philip, "Go to that chariot and stay near it."' Philip did as he was told and the outcome was the conversion and baptism of the Ethiopian eunuch, a seeker after truth.

The Holy Spirit has continued to lead or direct Christians to do ordinary and extraordinary things in order to share with others the good news concerning Jesus. Does this remind you of how someone shared the gospel with you? Or perhaps you remember an occasion when the Spirit directed you to knock at a front door which was opened by someone who subsequently became a Christian.

Acts 8:39: 'The Spirit of the Lord suddenly took Philip away, and the eunuch did not see him again, but went on his way rejoicing.' The evangelist's work was done, so the Spirit moved him on to proclaim the gospel elsewhere. There are lessons here regarding the leading and directing of the Holy Spirit. Philip was taken away, but the Ethiopian was not left to sink or swim on his own; we know that he loved the Scriptures, and we can be assured that, although he may not have had many, or any, fellow believers in Ethiopia, he found in God's word all the pastoral instruction that he needed for growth in discipleship. Today also, new converts need to get grounded in Scripture and to benefit from a spiritual shepherd's care. The shepherd will not necessarily be the evangelist who led the person to the Lord. After conversion accompaniment is an area which necessitates the guidance of the Holy Spirit.

Acts 13:1-4: 'Now in the church at Antioch there were prophets and teachers: Barnabas, Simeon called Niger, Lucius of Cyrene, Manaen (who had been brought up with Herod the tetrarch) and Saul. While they were worshipping the Lord and fasting, the Holy Spirit said, "Set apart for me Barnabas and Saul for the work to which I have called them." So after they had fasted and prayed, they placed their hands on them and sent them off. The two of them, sent on their way by the Holy Spirit, went . . .' This passage reports that 'the Holy Spirit **said**'; he **spoke** in order to lead and direct. Since there were prophets present in the worship service it seems probable that it was by the mouth of one or more of these that the Spirit spoke. The phraseology of the passage also suggests that the message was heard by all present. They united in further prayer and fasting, and then, presumably after a certain time waiting on the Lord, they placed their hands on the two called out men 'and sent them off'. This episode contains a wealth of instruction concerning the leading and directing of the Holy Spirit. He does speak, he does use prophets, he does ensure that entire communities are borne along and participate in the enterprise, he does enable the called out to go with assurance and conviction. You may be thinking that calls to service nowadays just do not happen in the way they did in the early church! Where are the prophets? Where are the communities that fast and pray? Where are the apostles like Barnabas and Saul? Let us reaffirm our conviction that God the Holy Spirit has not changed; he still speaks, by Scripture of course but also by prophets; yes, there are prophets in the church today!

Acts 16:6-7: 'Paul and his companions travelled throughout the region of Phrygia and Galatia, having been **kept by the Holy Spirit from preaching the word** in the province of Asia. When they came to the border of Mysia, they tried to enter Bithynia, but **the Spirit of Jesus would not allow them to**.'

These prohibitions ('kept . . . from', 'would not allow') are surprising, even perplexing, for many of us. We have been encouraged to go into the most difficult, dangerous and unreceptive places, but here we learn that the Spirit prevented Paul and his companions from going into certain regions. Why? We do not know the whole story, but one thing is clear . . . the Holy Spirit had another priority for the missionary team! After each prohibition they didn't turn back, they changed course to a more westerly direction. The Holy Spirit was progressively directing them to where they needed to go, i.e. to the port town Troas. There the Spirit led Paul by means of a nocturnal vision:

> *During the night Paul had a vision of a man of Macedonia standing and begging him, 'Come over to Macedonia and help us.' After Paul had seen the vision, we got ready at once to leave for Macedonia, concluding that God had called us to preach the gospel to them. (Acts 16:9-10)*

So it was that the gospel entered Europe. By means of a sequence of prohibitions, changes of direction and finally a clear call, the Holy Spirit led the team into Europe. Does the unwinding of this great missionary adventure imply that the initial plan to go into the Province of Asia and the next to enter Bithynia were both wrong, quite outside the will of God? We think not, for they set out to reach the un-evangelised and planned their route on that basis. But they were not rigid in their thinking; they were open to modification, correction and new un-anticipated revelation. So it was that the Spirit graciously, without reproof, led them a bit at a time to know and do the perfect will of God. They crossed the Aegean Sea, entered Macedonia and were used there to begin the wonderful, still ongoing work of evangelising Europe. God alone knows how many similar occasions of Holy Spirit leading have occurred throughout the world, with a mix of signals, sometimes go, sometimes stop and change direction, move on, stop and change direction again, now stay to witness and proclaim the message; the 'stay' being sometimes short, often lifelong, ending peaceably for most, but in martyrdom for others.

In his farewell words to the Ephesian elders Paul said, 'And now, **compelled by the Spirit**, I am going to Jerusalem, not knowing what will happen to me there. I only know that in every city **the Holy Spirit warns me** that prison and hardships are facing me' (Acts 20:22-23). Paul must have thought much of how his Master had felt compelled to go to Jerusalem (see Matthew 20:18 and Luke 9:51), but there was a big difference: Jesus knew very well what was to happen to him in that city. Paul was obedient to the Spirit's compulsions. He went to Jerusalem, and then to Rome. Through his final years the Spirit led him on. He experienced arrest and detention; trial by the Sanhedrin; plots to murder him; trials by governors Felix and Porcius Festus; an appearance before King Agrippa; a turbulent journey to Rome with storm, shipwreck and delays on the way. Arrival at Rome, he preached, was put under house arrest (maybe imprisonment) and then the final events, not reported in Acts, the nature of which, it seems, no one is absolutely sure, but tradition tells us of further imprisonment and martyrdom. Of many aspects of Paul's pilgrimage we can write with certainty, including his dependence on and obedience to the leading and direction of the Spirit.

Galatians 5:25: 'Since we live by the Spirit, let us keep in step with the Spirit.' The context of this exhortation in Galatians 5 is the fruit of the Spirit. Consequently, we must conclude that those in whom the Spirit produces fruit are also led by the Spirit, moving on in harmony with and at the same pace as the Holy Spirit.

Spirit-led believers and communities are mature and adult in Christ. Romans 8:14 tells us that 'those who are led by the Spirit of God are the children of God'. All who are in Christ are children of God, and most of us probably feel that we are but babes in Christ. However, Paul's assertion seems to imply that Christians who are Spirit led grow and mature and become adult sons and daughters of God; the implications do not escape us!

A warning to heed

The Holy Spirit is God; we very partially know him, his ways and his leading. Jesus likened him to the wind that blows wherever it pleases; you hear its sound, but you cannot tell where it comes from or where it is going. The Teacher (Ecclesiastes 11:5) gave us similar guidance: 'As you do not know the path of the wind . . . so you cannot understand the work of God, the Maker of all things.' Let us therefore adopt a-humble-and-ready-at-all-times-to-be-corrected attitude to our understanding of the Spirit's leading, guiding and directing. He will never fail us!

10

His Gifts

This is an enthralling subject! The chapters of scripture which particularly enlighten us on the nature and operation of these gifts are 12, 13 and 14 of 1 Corinthians. It seems that the matter of spiritual gifts was one of the several issues on which the Christians of the Corinthian community had sought guidance from the apostle Paul; he chose to reply in partnership with a brother named Sosthenes. Let us, as a starting point, quote verses 7-11 of their chapter 12 which identify nine gifts:

> *Now to each one the manifestation of the Spirit is given for the common good. To one there is given through the Spirit a message of wisdom, to another a message of knowledge by means of the same Spirit, to another faith by the same Spirit, to another gifts of healing by that one Spirit, to another miraculous powers, to another prophecy, to another distinguishing between spirits, to another speaking in different kinds of tongues, and to still another the interpretation of*

tongues. All these are the work of one and the same Spirit, and he distributes them to each one, just as he determines.

Nine gifts are listed. We may wonder, 'Is this list exhaustive?' Are there not other spiritual gifts, or God-given natural talents or skills, sanctified because consecrated to the Giver, which we could add to the list? We would acknowledge that all of us are guardians of such gifts, and they have vital roles in our lives and contributions in society and in the church. But we should ask another question: 'Is the list in 1 Corinthians about natural gifts, albeit sanctified, or is something else in view?' We note that most of the key words – wisdom, knowledge, faith, healing, miracles, tongues and interpretation – figure often in everyday human experience and parlance, and at first glance this could suggest that 1 Corinthians has in view Christ-centred, Spirit-sanctified, Bible-guided use of natural facilities. Many consider that this is how we should understand the passage cited above, and it is certainly important that we place all our talents and abilities at Jesus' feet. Others, perhaps not so many, believe that the passage is solely about Spirit-given, supernaturally operated gifts, in no way connected to natural facilities. Yet others consider that the giving and operation of each of the gifts is in some way a mix of the other two broad possibilities. Readers may be aware of other lines of thought and conviction. This leads us to state the obvious: the subject is not easy! What we must not do is close our eyes and hope that the matter will go away. Rather let us ask the Holy Spirit to open the eyes of our hearts, speaking to us from scripture and from the testimony of both the early church and the contemporary worldwide church militant.

As to whether or not the list is exhaustive we urge that our full attention and yearning be concentrated on the nine gifts mentioned prior to thinking of adding others. As the writers remind us, 'Jesus is Lord'. Let us be careful to acknowledge his Lordship in the area of spiritual gifts. In so doing we shall discover that 'God's love has been poured out into our hearts through the Holy Spirit, who he has given to us' (Romans 5:5). This reflection takes us to chapter 13 of 1 Corinthians, where we learn that love is the essential and indeed the only soil in which the seeds of spiritual gifts can germinate, take root and become mature plants that contribute divine health, vitality and understanding to the Lord's people. Therefore, the wise course on which we should embark, and continue, is that clearly signposted in 1 Corinthians 14:1: 'Follow the way of love and eagerly desire gifts of the Spirit.'

In 1 Corinthians 12:1 and 14:1 we find the Greek word *pneumatika* meaning 'spiritual things' or 'spirituals', but in most versions translated 'spiritual gifts'. This term seems to be used when an all-inclusive (all the gifts) sense is implied. Another Greek word, *charisma* (plural *'charismata'*), meaning 'gift of grace' or 'gift involving grace' is found in 1 Corinthians 12:4,9,28,30-31, 1 Timothy 4:14, 2 Timothy 1:6 and 1 Peter 4:10, where the subject is a specific gift. The emphasis on grace completely discounts any sense of merit in gifted persons; it also tells us that it is not solely the gifted ones who are the intended beneficiaries of the exercised gifts. Indeed not, for as 1 Corinthians 12:7 says, 'To each one the manifestation of the Spirit is given for the **common good**.' We understand this to mean primarily the community of believers, and secondarily unbelievers with whom the Christian community seeks to share the gospel of Jesus.

Many commentators note that the operation of spiritual gifts takes place in a relational context, i.e. most often within the family or fraternity of Christ's people (1 Corinthians 12:4-7), and also, but less often, within the context of love-motivated outreach to the unconverted, as Mark 16:20 implies: 'The disciples **went out** and preached everywhere, and the Lord worked with them and confirmed his word by the signs that accompanied it.' The 'signs' could well have been brought about by the operation of one or other of the gifts, e.g. gifts of healings. This is happening today, particularly in association with pioneering evangelism amongst hitherto unreached peoples.

Regarding the place for spiritual gifts in worship services, Harold Horton went so far as to write:

> *There can be no fully acceptable conformity to God's pattern of divine worship in a church where Spiritual Gifts are despised, or neglected, or abused. Spiritual Gifts are not an option in the Word. They are a positive essential, not only to service but also to worship. They are necessary avenues of revelation and necessary vehicles of adoration, without which no meeting for divine worship can be complete.*[47]

He also insisted on the 100 per cent supernatural character of each of the spiritual gifts.

Whilst we are not entirely comfortable with Horton's position, particularly regarding the operation of the gifts, it would be foolish to exclude such convictions from our own search for truth.

---

47. Harold Horton, *The Gifts of the Spirit*, (Springfield, MO: Gospel Publishing House, 1975), p.20.

We will now briefly share our thoughts on each of the nine gifts (1 Corinthians 12:8-10), mentioning a few instances of their operation; most of these are recorded in Acts, others come from contemporary experience.

'To one is given by the Spirit the word of wisdom' (KJV); 'Message of wisdom' (NIV)

The wisdom received by a believer in this way, by or through the Spirit, is not that which is acquired by a child from a parent's sound instruction or any other godly influence (see the early chapters of Proverbs), nor is it that which, by means of searching the scriptures, makes us 'wise for salvation through faith in Christ Jesus' (2 Timothy 3:15), but it is certainly not disassociated from these or any other form of God-given wisdom. Rather it is that God, who is all-wise, reveals by the Spirit a part of his wisdom to a believer for the benefit of the church and the progress of the Kingdom. It appears to be all about the revelation of hitherto hidden or not fully understood aspects of the unmeasurable wisdom of God.

Horton explains this gift as 'the supernatural revelation, by the Spirit, of Divine Purpose; the supernatural declaration of the Mind and Will of God; the supernatural unfolding of His Plans and Purposes concerning things, places, people: individuals, communities, nations'.[48]

Examples:
- Acts 10–16: here we learn of how the Spirit revealed the wisdom of God to Simon Peter, i.e. that by the

---

48. Harold Horton, *The Gifts of the Spirit*, p.56.

atoning sacrifice of his Son God offered salvation and inclusion not only to Jews but to all peoples, Jews and non-Jews alike. Shortly afterwards Peter, now a man with a new understanding, a new assurance, a new liberty, spoke this word of wisdom to his Gentile hosts, 'God has **shown me that** I should not call anyone impure or unclean' (Acts 10:28).

- Acts 15:15-21: here we are in the Council at Jerusalem; the Gentile question has been discussed. Peter, already convinced that God makes no distinction between Jew and Gentile, has spoken. Barnabas and Paul have added their testimony; it is now James' responsibility to sum up and make a recommendation. He does so with transparent and convincing wisdom, quoting Amos 9:11-12, adding, 'We should not make it difficult for the Gentiles who are turning to God [*by insisting on their being circumcised*].' His proposition was accepted, and the Gentiles were informed. There is no inkling here of supernatural revelation, but it was scriptural and spiritual, which helps us to understand that the conclusive message delivered by James to the Council was a 'word of wisdom', a revelation of the mind of God.

- Ephesians 1:9; 3:3-6: 'By the Spirit' Paul and the other apostles and prophets received the revelation 'not made known to people in other generations', that 'through the gospel the Gentiles are heirs together with Israel, members of one body, and sharers together in the promise in Christ Jesus'.

- Throughout the centuries many Christians have received clear revelation concerning the wisdom of God for their lives. These may not all have been due to an operation of the gift of the word of wisdom. But many probably were, especially, as in the case of Simon Peter, when the tenor of the revelation was diametrically opposed to the instinct and culture of the recipient.

'To another the word of knowledge by the same Spirit' (KJV); '... the message of knowledge by means of the same Spirit' (NIV)

God is both all-wise and all-knowing. That he desires to share elements of both these attributes with his redeemed people (in addition to matters already revealed in scripture) by means of the first two of the spiritual gifts is amazing. For Horton the operation of this gift is 'The supernatural revelation by the Holy Spirit of certain facts in the mind of God ... It is a divinely given fragment of divine knowledge ... It is knowledge miraculously conveyed.'[49]

Examples:
- Acts 9:11-12. The Lord knew where newly converted Saul was staying, the identity of the house owner, Saul's physical condition and what he needed to learn regarding God's purpose for his life, and he revealed all this knowledge to his disciple, Ananias, instructing him, despite his reluctance, to 'Go', telling him how to administer the 'Word' of divine knowledge he had received. Ananias obeyed, he

---

49. Harold Horton, *The Gifts of the Spirit*, pp.39-40.

ministered to Saul who was filled with the Holy Spirit, healed of blindness, baptised in water (v.15-18) and ushered into the role he was to fulfil for the rest of his days.

- From early in the 20th century many evangelists, and also leaders of local Christian communities, in many parts of the world, have received revelations from the Holy Spirit concerning the needs of persons in their congregations or encounters; needs such as sickness, moral and spiritual conditions, and other matters. Many consider that these revelations, and their subsequent transmission to the persons, or communities, in need, are manifestations of the gift of the word of knowledge. Many of the needy folk concerned have testified to the subsequent healing or deliverance or other help they received.

- Jamieson, Fausset and Brown (JFB) understand that the operation of this gift is 'the ready utterance supernaturally of truths already received'.[50] Whilst this may not be the only permissible approach, we feel constrained to accept it as one of the several manners of understanding the gift and the possible circumstances in which it operates.

- The spiritual gifts of the word of wisdom and the word of knowledge are closely related and complementary. Often, when considering a specific manifestation, we are aware of being in the presence of both divine wisdom and divine knowledge.

---

50. Jamieson, Fausset and Brown, *Commentary Practical and Explanatory on the Whole Bible* (London: Oliphants Ltd, 1961). p.1215.

'To another faith by the same Spirit'

This, in common with the other spiritual gifts, is not given to all believers; consequently, it is not that faith which God gives so graciously to all persons who, convicted of sin and their need of pardon, accept Jesus and the propitiatory sacrifice he made by his death, placing their faith in him as their Lord and Saviour. This faith is a gift of God freely available to all repentant sinners. Furthermore, it is not the faith we should have that God will fulfil his promises.

Commentators offer these thoughts:

> NIV study note: it is 'faith to meet a specific need within the body of Christ'.[51]
>
> Matthew Henry: it is a gift 'whereby they [the gifted ones] are enabled to trust God in any emergency'.[52]
>
> Jamieson, Fausset and Brown: it is not about 'doctrines, but of miracles: confidence in God, by the impulse of his Spirit, that he would enable them to perform any required miracle'.[53]

Examples:

- Acts chapters 27–28 tell the story of Paul's drama-filled journey, mostly by sea, from Caesarea to Rome. Soon after leaving Crete the ship was caught up in a violent storm which continued to rage for many days; the ship and all aboard were in grave danger, and finally they gave up all hope of coming

---

51. *NIV Study Bible* (London: Hodder & Stoughton, 1987), p.1716.
52. Matthew Henry, p.2266.
53. Jamieson, Fausset and Brown, p.1215.

through alive. Then a night came when an angel of God visited Paul to reassure him and to tell him that his life, and the lives of all sailing with him, would be saved. Come the morning Paul stood up and told the men what the angel had said to him. He then added, 'So keep up your courage, men, **for I have faith in God** that it will happen just as he told me' (Acts 27:25) or 'Sirs, be of good cheer: for I believe God, that it shall be even as it was told me' (KJV). It appears to us that Paul, in making this bold statement, exercised the gift of faith. This was faith of 'able to move mountains' character; a faith that made the normally impossible, possible, and even absolutely certain; a faith supernaturally inspired and guided. Nevertheless, no one on that ship was to have an easy time. The storm raged on; Paul had to be vigilant; discipline had to be maintained; good sense had its place. They spotted land ahead; the ship struck a sandbar and broke up; panic almost set in but Paul acted authoritatively, and 'everyone reached land in safety' (27:44). God had honoured the exercise of the gift of faith.

We have acknowledged the all-essential supernatural element in this operation of the gift, i.e. in Paul's declaration, but we should also take careful note of the subsequent good sense and Holy Spirit-anointed authority that enabled the word of faith to produce a perfectly admirable conclusion. We also suggest that the raising to life of two deceased persons, Dorcas (Acts 9:36-43) and Eutychus (Acts 20:7-12), may well have been operations of the gift of faith.

'To another the gifts of healing by the same Spirit' (KJV); 'To another gifts of healing by that one Spirit' (NIV)

A literal translation of the Greek reads 'gifts of healings'. An NIV study note comments: 'The double plural may suggest different kinds of illnesses and the various ways God heals them.'[54]

Accounts of pioneering evangelism in the Book of Acts tell us that healing the sick accompanied the proclamation of the gospel: e.g. the crippled beggar at the gate called Beautiful (3:1-26), paralytics and cripples in Samaria (8:4-8), a paralytic named Aeneas who had been bedridden for eight years (9:32-35), a man in Lystra, lame from birth who had never walked (14:8-10), the chief official of Malta's father who was suffering from fever and dysentery, followed by the rest of the sick on the island (28:7-9).

No doubt these gifts were also regularly in operation within local Christian communities. James wrote to the believers of the diaspora encouraging them, when sick, to 'call the elders of the church to pray over them and anoint them with oil in the name of the Lord. And the prayer offered in faith will make the sick person well' (James 5:14-15). This exhortation envisages a corporate ministry exercised together by the local elders, but, then and now, it was and still is helpful and beneficial for the eldership team to have one or more members who have received gifts of healings.

Whilst there are only sparse written accounts of the widespread exercise of gifts of healings after the early church period, it seems very probable that we shall learn, when we reach our heavenly home, that these gifts have

---

54. *NIV Study Bible*, p.1716.

never been absent from evangelistic and church ministry. It is certain that these gifts are very much in operation today in many parts of the world, both in association with the propagation of the gospel and within local Christian communities. Mark 16:18 tells us that those who believe will, in Jesus' name, 'place their hands on people who are ill, and they will get well'.

'To another the working of miracles' (KJV); 'To another miraculous powers' (NIV)

A literal translation of the original text gives 'deeds of power'. This suggests that the operation of this gift brings about humanly inexplicable change. An NIV study note reads: 'In scripture a miracle is an action that cannot be explained by natural means. It is an act of God intended as an evidence of his power and purpose.'[55] With his habitual concise simplicity Cruden explained that a miracle is 'a supernatural occurrence produced by the power of God'.[56]

It may be correct to understand that the Holy Spirit-imparted gifts of faith, healings and working of miracles overlap to some extent, particularly in regard to healings; however, our Bibles contain reports of miraculous operations of the Spirit that are not healings.

It seems probable that the driving out of demons involves primarily the gifts of faith and the working of miracles, followed where necessary (and this is often the case) by the healing of associated emotional, psychological and physical hurts.

---

55. NIV Study Bible, p.1716.
56. Alexander Cruden, *Cruden's Complete Concordance to the Bible* (Cambridge: The Lutterworth Press, 1977), p.434.

The Old and New Testaments contain many accounts of miracles that had nothing to do with healings. From the story of the dividing of the Red Sea waters to that of Jesus calming the life-threatening, storm-torn waters of Lake Galilee, readers' powers of conception are stretched to their limits. We find ourselves walking with confidence and assurance, alongside the Israelites, on the dry bed of the sea, and standing amongst the disciples in the ship, feeling overwhelmingly relieved and looking out in admiration and gratitude over the calm surface of the lake.

Should we believe God for similar miracles today? Surely scripture, and the many faith-filled testimonies it contains, challenge us to expect the inexplicable, the miraculous. Is this not why God has provided this gift entitled 'the working of miracles'?

Here are two texts that can encourage Christians to earnestly desire this gift:

- Galatians 3:5: 'Does God give you his Spirit and work miracles among you by the works of the law, or by your believing what you heard?' Here Christians are called to believe for miracles.

- Hebrews 2:3-4: 'This salvation, which was first announced by the Lord, was confirmed to us by those who heard him. God also testified to it by signs, wonders and various miracles, and by gifts of the Holy Spirit distributed according to his will.' Am I, are you, among those in the church that God has appointed to be 'workers of miracles'?

Examples from Acts:

Stephen, the deacon who was to become the first Christian martyr, was 'a man full of God's grace and power, [who] performed great wonders and signs among the people' (6:8). Philip, another deacon and evangelist, 'went down to a city in Samaria and proclaimed the Messiah there. When the crowds heard Philip and saw the signs he performed, they all paid close attention to what he said. For with shrieks, impure spirits came out of many, and many who were paralysed or lame were healed. So there was great joy in that city' (8:5-8). A local man, a sorcerer named Simon, 'Believed and was baptised. And he followed Philip everywhere, astonished by the great signs and miracles he saw' (8:13).

During the previously mentioned Council of Christian leaders held at Jerusalem 'the whole assembly became silent as they listened to Barnabas and Paul telling about the signs and wonders God had done among the Gentiles through them' (15:12). Later, Paul, finally safe on Malta and enjoying the local hospitality, whilst gathering firewood was bitten by a poisonous snake. He shook the viper off; the locals expected him to die but he suffered no ill effects (28:1-6). That was a miracle, maybe an operation of both the gift of faith and of the working of miracles (see Mark 16:18).

'To another prophecy'

Prophecy we understand to be the declaration by a believer of a revelation of the mind of God, supernaturally received from the Holy Spirit. Peter, quoting the prophet Joel, said, on the day of Pentecost, that prophecy is for the last days; in other words, it is for now!

The ascended Lord Jesus places ministries in his church; these are mentioned in Ephesians 4:11, the first two being apostles and prophets. These often minister in tandem, e.g. Paul (apostle) and Silas (prophet). The prophet's role was wide in scope, and potentially still is, including prediction (Agabus, Acts 11:27-28; 21:10-11) and communication of God's plans and directions as to how these were to be accomplished. Acts 13:1-3 is a clear account of how the Holy Spirit directed the church at Antioch, probably via the prophets present in that community, to set apart Barnabas and Paul for the work to which the Lord had called them. Timothy too was the subject of directive prophecy: 'I am giving you this command in keeping with the prophecies once made about you' (1 Timothy 1:18); 'Do not neglect your gift, which was given you through prophecy when the body of elders laid their hands on you' (4:14). Acts conveys the impression that prophets then were not numerous, but their ministry was of crucial importance.

However, our present concern is not the office, or ministry, of prophet which was and is exercised by a few, but the gift of prophecy which all believers are exhorted to eagerly desire. 'Follow the way of love and eagerly desire gifts of the Spirit, especially the gift of prophecy' (1 Corinthians 14:1). Paul would have everyone in the Corinthian church prophesying (v.5)! Verse 3 sets out the scope of the gift; it reads, 'The one who prophesies speaks to people for their strengthening, encouraging and comfort.' No mention of prediction, or foretelling, or revelation, or directives, for these functions are, unless the Holy Spirit wills otherwise in particular circumstances, the domain of the prophet and sometimes the apostle (see Ephesians 3:5).

A local Christian community is rich indeed if it has several persons exercising a gift of prophecy. We have no record in scripture of messages which were delivered by persons exercising this gift, but there are many passages in Acts and the letters that tell of Christians in daily need of strengthening, encouragement and comfort. As a sample case please take a look at Hebrews 12 which tells us that the letter's recipients were having a hard time: they were experiencing the rigors of discipleship (v.7-11), their arms were feeble and their legs weak (v.12) and perhaps they were also suffering persecution from the world around them. The writer exhorts, encourages and comforts them by directing their attention to Jesus who had suffered so much for them (v.1-6); his was the example to follow. We know that it is the Holy Spirit's role to draw Jesus' disciples' attention to their Master (John 16:14-15), and one of the means of communication the Spirit uses is to speak to us via the gift of prophecy; in this way the Spirit and the Son jointly minister strength, encouragement and comfort to the Father's children.

The only identification in Acts of persons gifted in this way is in chapter 21:9: 'He [Philip the evangelist/deacon] had four unmarried daughters who prophesied.' Philip, and presumably his daughters, lived in Caesarea. We can imagine the rich blessings their local Christian assembly enjoyed through their prophetic ministries. My wife, our family and I have, through several decades, been part of local churches in which the prophetic flow has, though not always abundant, graciously contributed to the community's life and ministry. Whilst the operation of the prophetic gift is primarily for believers (1 Corinthians 14:22), we are told in verses 24-25 that it can have a decisive impact on the unsaved, contributing to their conversion.

The orderly manner in which persons exercising this gift should minister, and the mutual control that all prophets must exercise, are clearly set out in verses 29-33. For example, verse 29: 'Two or three prophets should speak, and the others should weigh carefully what is said.'

'To another discerning of spirits' (KJV); 'To another distinguishing between spirits' (NIV)

This gift has to do with discerning or distinguishing between that which is of the Spirit and that which is of the world; that which is of God and that which is of Satan. This said we may be tempted to think that simple good sense, or Spirit-sanctified sense, should, on almost all occasions, suffice for discernment between what is of God and what is not (see 1 John 4:1-6, which exhorts us along these lines). This is certainly so, but most Christians would acknowledge that their day-by-day walk brings them regularly to situations where discernment necessitates something more than sanctified, Scripture-guided sense. We have in mind distinguishing between certain forms of physical or mental illness and possession by evil spirits, between true and false prophesies, between true and false claims, allegations and assertions, and many another concoction or deception of satanic conception including occult practices.

Horton, faithful to his overall approach to the gifts of the Spirit, declares this gift to be 'a gift of revelation, entirely supernatural in operation; its focus too is on the supernatural ... the realm of spirits'.

JFB state that this gift is about 'discerning between the operation of God's Spirit and the evil spirit'.

Examples:

- Acts 16:16-18: the Spirit revealed to Paul, and perhaps to those accompanying him, that the persistent hecklings of a slave girl were, although true, inspired by an evil spirit by whom she was possessed; the evil spirit's purpose being to deceptively get the better of Paul. At Paul's command, in the name of Jesus Christ, 'The spirit left her.'

- 1 Timothy 4:1-5: the Holy Spirit gives Paul discernment concerning deceiving spirits that were leading believers into error, moral and spiritual bondage.

One day, probably soon, Jesus will come back to earth, and we will be 'gathered to him' (2 Thessalonians 2:1). Prior to his coming rebellion will occur and 'the lawless one' will be revealed; this will be a time when Satan will exhibit 'all sorts of displays of power through signs and wonders that serve the lie, and all the ways that wickedness deceives those who are perishing' (2:9-10). During this period, it will be especially important for Christian communities to benefit from the exercise of the Holy Spirit-bestowed gift of discerning, or distinguishing, of spirits.

'To another divers kinds of tongues' (KJV); 'To another speaking in different kinds of tongues' (NIV)

A Christian friend, the wife of a pastor, testified to us that regularly praying to the Lord in tongues during her personal devotions is a source to her of great comfort and blessing. No doubt this lady began speaking and praying in tongues when she was baptised in/with the Holy Spirit. Paul's written testimony to the Christians at Corinth is very similar. He wrote to the Corinthians, seemingly referring to his personal prayer life, 'I thank God that I speak in tongues more than all of you' (1 Corinthians 14:18).

And it seems probable that he too began when he was filled with the Holy Spirit, which occurred when Ananias laid hands on him in the house on Straight Street, Damascus (Acts 9). Reflecting on how Paul probably felt whilst in prison, after beatings, being left for dead, being misunderstood and suffering insult because of his attachment to Jesus, as well as on the many occasions when praying before retiring for sleep and rest after having had the immense joy of leading individuals, families and communities to Christ, would it not have been normal and appropriate for him to speak to the Lord in tongues? Today this is still the common and usual experience of Spirit-baptised believers.

Nevertheless, wonderful and beneficent as 'tongues' are in personal communion with the Lord, this is not the same as the gift of diverse tongues for ministry in the church, which Paul explains in chapters 12–14. There are occasions when the exercise of this gift is in a language unknown to the speaker but known to certain of the hearers present. One time my wife and I were present in a meeting when a message was delivered in Arabic, a language unknown to the speaker. A young man, an Arab, heard and understood the message, and this contributed to his being drawn to the Saviour. This was reminiscent of that special day of Pentecost at Jerusalem. However, for the most part, exercise of this gift is by means of a tongue, or language, unknown to both speaker and hearers alike. Consequently, it operates in union with the complementary **gift of interpretation of tongues**, i.e. interpretation into the native language of the people present. This is the situation envisaged in 1 Corinthians, and it implies that persons possessing one or other of the two gifts need to be constantly 'in the Spirit', in harmony with the Lord Jesus, the Holy Spirit, each other and other believers of the community, in order to be ready at all times to minister in tandem.

The scope of the combined ministry of the two gifts is the same as that of the gift of prophecy. This is made clear in 1 Corinthians 14:5: 'The one who prophesies is greater than the one who speaks in tongues, unless someone interprets, so that the church may be edified.' We should also note that persons gifted to deliver a message in a tongue should themselves pray that they may interpret (v.13).

Scripture does not contain any records of interpretation of tongues, but on many occasions throughout church history, particularly from the early 1900s onwards, assembled believers have been enriched by the exercise of the two gifts. In our experience the enriching is particularly present during times of corporate worship.

Jesus said that one of the signs that will accompany those who believe is 'they will speak in new tongues' (Mark 16:17).

How the gifts are received

The writers repeatedly encourage the Corinthian Christians to persist in their desire to possess spiritual gifts; we have already noted the phrases 'eagerly desire the greater gifts' and 'follow the way of love and eagerly desire spiritual gifts'. These exhortations place the onus on each of the readers – personally and collectively. The motivating force must be love: love for each other, love for the unconverted, including adversaries and enemies, as so beautifully explained in 1 Corinthians 13 and Matthew 5:43-48.

Earnest prayer and seeking of the Lord, purification of motives and understanding the will of God are called for. The reception of a gift may then be manifested during a time of personal devotion, or in a small group, or when the local church is assembled for worship, or when believers are confronted by a particular need.

The body of elders and Paul the apostle were used by the Spirit, by means of their laying on of hands, to convey to Timothy a spiritual gift. A prophetic message accompanied this endowment.

The Holy Spirit is still endowing today. On a worldwide scale our ascended Saviour still gives to the church ministers who with Paul say, 'I long to see you so that I may impart to you some spiritual gift to make you strong' (Romans 1:11).

One of L.F.W. Woodford's hymns, sung to the tune St Matthias:[57]

> *Lord Jesus, thou thy church hast graced*
> *With gifts supernal and divine;*
> *Gifts of thy Spirit, pure and chaste,*
> *With heavenly lustre here to shine.*
> *Ascending to thy Father's throne,*
> *Thou hast bestowed them on thine own.*

---

[57]. L.F.W. Woodford, 'Lord Jesus, thou thy church hast graced', *Redemption Hymnal* (1955), hymn 242.

In thee, our living head, are stored
Treasures of wisdom, light and love;
On us, thy members, thou hast poured
This wealth of blessing from above.
Oh, may we prove, this very hour,
The nine-fold splendour of thy power.

Speak, Lord! By word of wisdom pure,
Thy will reveal, thy mind impart;
By word of knowledge, swift and sure,
Illume, instruct, and guide each heart.
So shall we trace thy way divine,
Line upon line, in clear design.

Thy mighty faith on us bestow,
Beyond our measure or our thought;
Let gifts of healing from thee flow,
And wonders in thy name be wrought.
Make bare thine arm, confirm thy word,
That all may own thee Christ and Lord!

Touch thou our lips! We would aspire
To speak the praises of thy love,
Gifted with pure prophetic fire
And holy unction from above;
Whilst, through thy searching Spirit, taught
The secret springs of life and thought.

With tongues of men or seraph strain,
Speak forth thy words, in praise, in prayer;
Then make each heaven-sent message plain,
That we thy glories may declare.
Grace every gift with love's high theme:
Yea, reign o'er all, O love supreme!

11

His Fruit

It's mid-afternoon and I've just enjoyed eating a tangerine; the colour of the fruit, outside and inside, was attractive, the taste was excellent which, together with the firm texture, made for a pleasant in-the-mouth experience; the peel will go into the compost bin which will ensure its extended usefulness, and I feel quite pleased with myself for having responded to one of today's healthy eating slogans . . . five fruit or veg a day! I didn't really have all these thoughts in mind when I took the fruit from the bowl and rapidly devoured it; no, I functioned like an automaton. The calorific, vitamin and other characteristics of the fruit were not in my mind; I saw the tangerine, liked the idea that it immediately provoked, took it and ate it.

It's not only the proof of the pudding that is in the eating, it is also that of the fruit. Whilst it is true that a great deal has been beneficially said and written about the fruit (we often say 'fruits') of the Spirit, we will all acknowledge that there is nothing better than feeding on these fruits as God offers them to us through sisters and brothers in the body of Christ. At this point I am wondering whether it is useful trying to explain the fruit, or fruits, of the Spirit. Surely everyone understands what they are about? Consequently, we will endeavour to be circumspect in what we write, and concentrate on emphasising the essential fact, i.e. that the fruit with which we are concerned is the fruit produced by the Holy Spirit.

Quite a few years before the fruit of the Spirit became a subject about which Paul and others wrote, Jesus laid down the simple but essential guidelines regarding fruit-bearing that his disciples would need to assimilate and to never let slip from their minds. During the course of the teaching he gave whilst seated on a Palestinian mountainside, the Master spoke of good fruit and bad fruit; the former grows on good trees, the latter on bad. Simple! Let us listen again to the wise counsel of our Teacher.

> *Watch out for false prophets. They come to you in sheep's clothing, but inwardly they are ferocious wolves. By their fruit you will recognise them. Do people pick grapes from thorn-bushes, or figs from thistles? Likewise, every good tree bears good fruit, but a bad tree bears bad fruit. A good tree cannot bear bad fruit, and a bad tree cannot bear good fruit. Every tree that does not bear good fruit is cut down and thrown into the fire. Thus, by their fruit you will recognise them.*
>
> *Not everyone who says to me, 'Lord, Lord,' will enter the kingdom of heaven, but only the one who does the will of my Father who is in heaven. Many will say to me on that day, 'Lord, Lord, did we not prophesy in your name and in your name drive out demons and*

in your name perform many miracles?' Then I will tell them plainly, 'I never knew you. Away from me, you evildoers!' (Matthew 7:15-23)

These are very solemn, even mortifying, words, particularly the second paragraph, which we all need to apply to ourselves trusting in Christ and the Holy Spirit to render our works pure and acceptable to God. Regarding the first paragraph, in the light of Scripture as a whole which gives us to understand that since the nature possessed by each and every human being is corrupt, sinful and 'bad' we are all by nature 'bad trees' bearing 'bad fruit'. Romans 3:10-12 begins, 'There is no one righteous, not even one.' It is only by regeneration (new birth), and the subsequent indwelling of the Holy Spirit and his sanctifying work, that redeemed men and women become 'good trees' bearing 'good fruit'. Paul summarised this in his first letter to the Corinthians 6:11 (please read verses 9-11), reminding his readers that 'that is what some of you were. **But** you were washed, you were sanctified, you were justified in the name of the Lord Jesus Christ and by the Spirit of our God'. This is grace indeed; no credit to either the Corinthians or us for we are not different from them.

Bearing in mind these guidelines laid down by Jesus let us move on to the best-known Bible passage on the fruit of the Spirit: Galatians 5:22-23.

But the fruit of the Spirit is love, joy, peace, forbearance, kindness, goodness, faithfulness, gentleness and self-control. Against such things there is no law.

The conjunction 'but' calls our attention to a catalogue of 'acts of the sinful nature', which the author of the letter has just set out (v.19-21, see also 1 Corinthians 6:9-10, Ephesians 5:3-7) in order to show that they are the very opposite of the acts produced by the fruit of the Spirit. Paul has explained that there is an enormous difference between the acts ('bad fruit') that un-regenerated human nature produces, and those which persons who are regenerated by the Spirit, and who live by the Spirit, produce. Paul writes, 'Live by the Spirit, and you will not gratify the desires of the flesh' (Galatians 5:16). Then, after describing both the acts of the flesh (i.e. the sinful nature) and the fruit of the Spirit, he powerfully reminds us that believers are constantly engaged in a spiritual and moral conflict between the nature with which they were born and the new nature ('Christ in us') they received at their new birth. He writes, 'Those who belong to Christ Jesus have crucified the flesh with its passions and desires. Since we live by the Spirit, let us keep in step with the Spirit. Let us not become conceited, provoking and envying each other' (5:24-26). This is a conflict in which we shall be engaged for the rest of our lives! Courage, sisters and brothers, life is mercifully short!

Paul was well placed for dispensing clear teaching on this subject, for he was well aware that, prior to his encounter with the Lord Jesus, his legalistic deeds of unkindness and destruction against followers of 'the Way' were the fruit of his unholy human nature, whereas after that encounter, which was when his experience of saving and sanctifying grace began, the Holy Spirit started to produce in him the fruit that disseminates love and all the rest.

We note that the Galatians text is about 'the fruit' not 'the fruits'; we may like to think of 'the fruit' as a unique fruit having many flavours, nine being identified, each of which becomes apparent as and when the need arises. A given circumstance may be the occasion for just one of the flavours to be in evidence; another may call for more than one of the flavours to be manifested, but very often all nine will have a vital role to fulfil. This probably strikes us as more than challenging, and frankly unattainable, since it implies perfection. Many of us find comfort, even a sense of security, in saying that nobody is perfect, and that perfection cannot be known this side of the grave. But is that the whole truth? After all, Jesus very plainly said, 'Be perfect . . . as your heavenly Father is perfect' (Matthew 5:48).

Christian perfection was taught, and presumably still is, within the Holiness movement and elsewhere; it was powerfully proclaimed by the Wesley brothers. Is it not time that Christians revisited this subject, praying that the Spirit reveal to us (the church), from Scripture, the mind of God on the matter? In the meantime, we can all make progress in the right direction by praying that the fruit the Spirit produces in us, individually and collectively, a rich and full panoply of the potential flavours.

There are a number of sylvan metaphors in the Bible which help us to better understand our potential in God as believers and disciples:

Isaiah 61:3: 'They will be called **oaks of righteousness**, a planting of the LORD for the display of his splendour.' The Lord makes his people strong, sturdy, useful and admirable.

Psalm 92:12-14: 'The righteous will flourish **like a palm tree**, they will grow **like a cedar of Lebanon**, planted in the house of the LORD, they will flourish in the courts of our God. They will still bear fruit in old age, they will stay fresh and green.' Made righteous by Jesus, his disciples grow straight and strong; integrity and enduring freshness are their hallmarks.

Psalm 1:3: 'That person [whose delight is in the law of the Lord] is like **a tree planted by streams of water**, which yields its fruit in season and whose leaf does not wither.' It is the Lord's pleasure to constantly resource those who delight in him.

In the imagery of our subject believers are like fruit trees. With which species of fruit tree would you want to be likened? If you accept the line of thinking set out thus far you will find identifying with an appropriate tree challenging, and more . . . impossible! Where in the world is there a tree that produces a fruit possessing nine different tastes which, nevertheless, are not totally dissimilar and, amazingly, blend very deliciously together? Regenerated persons are, each and every one, new creations, fearfully and wonderfully made. God the Holy Spirit dwells within them all, and it is he who enables them, the trees of the Lord, to be extraordinarily productive. Indeed, it is the Spirit who has been actively present throughout each tree's life, from seed germination, through early growth and root development to maturity, providing protection, nourishment and nurture. The Spirit also works in believers' lives in other ways that have a parallel in the world of fruit tree growing, for example pruning in order to eliminate deadwood, wild or potentially unproductive shoots, treatments to eliminate disease or rectify damage inflicted by inclement weather, animals or fire. The aim of the fruit tree grower is to produce perfect fruit; the aim of the Spirit for believers is nothing less. God's trees are so precious and important to him.

Readers may well be thinking of one or two rather different biblical metaphors; for example, the beautiful image we find in John chapter 15. Here Jesus is the root and stem of the vine, and his disciples are the branches who produce fruit solely because they are connected to the living Christ, thereby receiving life, energy and all things necessary from him for being fruitful. With gratitude we sing, 'My soul is now united to Christ, the living vine.'[58] The Father (the Holy Spirit working with him) is the vine-grower, keeper and carer; it is he who prunes, makes the rain to fall and the sun to shine on the vineyard, and protects the vines when in bloom from being ravaged by prowling little foxes (Song of Songs 2:15). All this in order to bring about what Jesus said, 'This is to my Father's glory, that you bear much fruit, showing yourselves to be my disciples' (John 15:8).

Another appropriate figure is that of the in-grafted branches (see Romans 11:11-24). Here believers, particularly Gentiles, are wild olive branches which have been grafted into the community of God's people, 'a cultivated olive tree', which makes them able to produce good fruit.

Submission to the Spirit, yielding to him, obedience, love and devotion to him are called for.

James Mountain has given us these thoughts:

> *Thrice-blessed Spirit! Giver of salvation,*
> *Purchased by Jesus on the cross of shame;*
> *Dwell in our hearts; transform them with thy beauty*
> *Fairest adorning of our Saviour's name.*

---

58. Hugh Bourne (1772–1852), William Sanders (b.1779), 'My soul is now united to Christ, the living vine', https://hymnary.org/hymn/SBSA1986/361 (accessed 1.4.24).

Thy nine-fold grace bestow upon us freely;
Love, deep and full, to God and all mankind;
Joy in the Lord, 'mid every earthly sorrow;
Peace, calm and sweet, that guardeth heart and mind.

Make us longsuffering, 'mid earth's provocations;
Gentleness gives us, when enduring wrong;
Goodness impart, that we e'en foes may succour;
Faithfulness grant, to change our toil to song.

Meekness bestow, with humble self-abasement,
And self-control, through thy controlling might;
And as we list to every call of duty,
May we do all as in thy searching sight.

Then with the gift of holiness within us;
We not less human, but made more divine;
Our lives replete with heaven's supernal beauty,
Ever declare – that beauty Lord is thine.[59]

James Mountain was a pastor and evangelist; as a hymnist he often wrote both the words and the music. In the last verse of this hymn he surely struck the right note in ascribing to the Lord all the beauty of the fruit produced in believers by the Holy Spirit. In a very beautiful mixed metaphor Paul calls upon us to 'live as children of the light (for the fruit of the light consists in all goodness, righteousness and truth) and find out what pleases the Lord' (Ephesians 5:8-10).

Should it be that you find the notion of nine different, but harmonious, 'flavours' or 'tastes' unattractive, possible alternatives or synonyms are: 'graces', 'virtues' or 'attributes.

---

59. James Mountain (1844–1933), 'Thrice blessed Spirit! Giver of salvation', https://hymnary.org/tune/thrice_blessed_spirit_giver_of_mountain (accessed 1.4.24).

For example, in Colossians 3:12-14 we find that many of the fruit virtues which are a disciple's 'clothing'. In 2 Peter 1:5-9 these virtues, or fruit flavours, are set forth as qualities which believers should possess 'in increasing measure'.

We have stated our reluctance to elaborate on the nine characteristics of the fruit of the Spirit identified in the letter to the Galatians. However, for readers who feel that this leaves a gap in our approach to the subject we propose an extract from Adam Clarke's commentary, written in the early 19th century:

Love – Αγαπη· An intense desire to please God, and to do good to mankind; the very soul and spirit of all true religion; the fulfiling of the law, and what gives energy to faith itself.

Joy – Χαρα· The exultation that arises from a sense of God's mercy communicated to the soul in the pardon of its iniquities, and the prospect of that eternal glory of which it has the foretaste in the pardon of sin. See Romans 5:2.

Peace – Ειρηνη· The calm, quiet, and order, which take place in the justified soul, instead of the doubts, fears, alarms, and dreadful forebodings, which every true penitent less or more feels, and must feel till the assurance of pardon brings peace and satisfaction to the mind . . .

Long-suffering – Μακροθυμια· Long-mindedness, bearing with the frailties and provocations of others, from the consideration that God has borne long with ours . . . bearing up also through all the troubles and difficulties of life without murmuring or repining;

submitting cheerfully to every dispensation of God's providence ...

Gentleness – Χρηστοτης· Benignity, affability; a very rare grace, often wanting in many who have a considerable share of Christian excellence. A good education and polished manners, when brought under the influence of the grace of God, will bring out this grace with great effect.

Goodness – Αγαϑωσυνη· The perpetual desire and sincere study, not only to abstain from every appearance of evil, but to do good to the bodies and souls of men to the utmost of our ability ....

Faith – Πιστις, here used for fidelity – punctuality in performing promises, conscientious carefulness in preserving what is committed to our trust, in restoring it to its proper owner, in transacting the business confided to us, neither betraying the secret of our friend, nor disappointing the confidence of our employer.

Meekness – Πραοτης· Mildness, indulgence toward the weak and erring, patient suffering of injuries without feeling a spirit of revenge, an even balance of all tempers and passions, the entire opposite to anger.

Temperance – Εγκρατεια· Continence, self-government, or moderation, principally with regard to sensual or animal appetites. Moderation in eating, drinking, sleeping, etc.[60]

---

60. Adam Clarke, *Commentary on Galatians* (CreateSpace Independent Publishing Platform, 2015), Kindle Edition, locations 1405-1433.

When London tasted the fruit of the Spirit

In the summer of 1952, at the beginning of my student days in London, I became a Christian. Happily, I got to know a number of fervent and evangelically active believers, principally in two local churches of different denominations. Looking back I recollect that many Christians were busy enough within their denominational boundaries, but fellowship and united outreach outside these limits were not very common, although certainly not non-existent. Then came a gradual but palpable change; preparations for the 1954 Greater London Crusade began. Christians from many and varied church associations came together to pray, to organise, to train for functioning as counsellors, stewards or choral singers. By the time the Crusade meetings began at Harringay Arena, with Billy Graham as the principal speaker, expectations and enthusiasm amongst believers were very strong; unity in Christ Jesus was very present; a longing that many would come to know Jesus as their personal Saviour was infectiously touching thousands of persons; London for Christ was the vision. Unity, harmony, joy in serving Jesus, common purpose and pleasure in working together in the sharing of the gospel with the people of the capital (and the provinces for the impact of the crusade became wider and wider) were all very much in evidence, and great blessing was experienced inside and around many local churches. Folk in all walks of life were touched by the grace of God, and this continued over an extended period. Clear and powerful preaching, effective publicity, generous giving and especially fervent believing prayer all played important roles. Looking back, one feels sure that the most powerful impact on the public was via the fruit of the Spirit evident in the lives of believers and Christian communities alike.

Fanny J. Crosby's song 'Rescue the perishing' is couched in 19th-century language which Christians today would probably not use, but she certainly writes effectively of the Holy Spirit fruit of love and kindness which are always present when the Lord's people are walking in step with the Spirit:

> *Rescue the perishing,*
> *Care for the dying,*
> *Snatch them in pity from sin and the grave*
> *Weep o'er the erring one,*
> *Lift up the fallen,*
> *Tell them of Jesus, the Mighty to save.*
>
> *Down in the human heart,*
> *Crushed by the tempter,*
> *Feelings lie buried that grace can restore;*
> *Touched by a **loving** heart,*
> *Wakened by **kindness**,*
> *Chords that were broken will vibrate once more.*[61]

The Toronto Blessing

We feel constrained to write a few lines regarding the Toronto Blessing (TB), which is the popular name given to the Christian awakening which began in 1994 at the Toronto Airport Vineyard Church. TB is rooted in the charismatic movement which has brought much good to

---

61. Fanny Crosby (1869), 'Rescue the perishing, care for the dying', https://hymnary.org/text/rescue_the_perishing_care_for_the_dying (accessed 1.4.24).

the Church Universal and to the world. Vineyard and TB have brought to many Christians growth in their knowledge and experience of the Holy Spirit.

However, we feel duty bound to strike a note of warning having been in fellowship up to the mid-90s with churches in Brussels where two families, perhaps more, became practitioners of TB-style worship, including flag waving (not a big problem) and imitation of animals, in voice and in mobility/movement (unacceptable to most of the members, the leaders being split on the issue). My wife and I now reside at some distance from Brussels where, to the best of our knowledge, TB is not present, although Vineyard is present.

Bible references to the nine characteristics of the fruit of the Spirit

Love

We know Paul's Spirit-inspired essay on love as chapter 13 of his first letter to the Corinthian church. It is sublime, and we encourage our readers to read it now. We note that chapters 12 and 14 of this letter teach us about some of the supernatural and powerful workings of the Holy Spirit. Chapter 13 implies that the greatest work of the Spirit in the lives of people is to generate love. Verse 13: 'These three remain: faith, hope and love. But the greatest of these is love [*agape*].' The remaining eight characteristics are rooted in and grow out of this *agape* love.

'Hope does not put us to shame, because God's love has been poured out into our hearts through the Holy Spirit, who has been given to us' (Romans 5:5). Christians visit our localities and then, their mission done, they move on. Inevitably they share news concerning our assembly with others. So it was that a certain Epaphras, a pioneering minister of Christ who visited Colosse, where he shared the gospel with the inhabitants, some of whom 'understood God's grace in all its truth' (Colossians 1:6 NIV 1984) and believed. The believers grew quickly and were soon 'bearing fruit'. A little later, when visiting Rome, Epaphras told Paul and Timothy of the Colossians' 'love in the Spirit'. That was a delightful testimony concerning the fruit of the Spirit.

Joy

Romans 14:17: 'For the kingdom of God is . . . righteousness, peace and joy in the Holy Spirit.'

Acts 13:52: 'And the disciples were filled with joy and with the Holy Spirit.' This is written of disciples who were experiencing persecution.

1 Peter 1:8-9 describes in effervescent, overflowing terms the joy that salvation in Jesus Christ produces. 'Though you have not seen him, you love him; and even though you do not see him now, you believe in him and are filled with an inexpressible and glorious joy, for you are receiving the end result of your faith, the salvation of your souls.' This is Holy Spirit-generated joy.

Peace

By the new birth persons formerly at enmity with God are bought into a relationship of 'peace with God' (Romans 5:1). By the grace of God, Christians allow the peace of

God to rule in their hearts. The dove is an emblem of peace and of the Holy Spirit. The Spirit of peace abode on Jesus the Messiah. He abides on the believer. He sanctifies and purifies, and his abiding presence ensures that the peace of God emanates from the believer to touch all around. It is by 'Christ in us' and the indwelling Spirit that Jesus' disciples become peacemakers (Matthew 5:9, see also Romans 14:17).

Patience

As the popular saying reminds us, patience certainly is a virtue, and probably most of us are acutely aware that we are deficient in this area. With admiration and gratitude we recollect the patience and perseverance of others with us: our parents (perhaps not our siblings!), our teachers (especially those who did their best to get us to learn another language), our sports coaches, our first employers and our spouses! Indwelling Spirit fostered patience (with perseverance) is extraordinary; it enables the believer to continue working the soil, sowing the seed, praying for germination and even leaving this world, apparently without an answer from God, for others to take on the responsibility of praying through to victory. In the citation below, we note that James emphasises the close link of compassion and mercy to patience and perseverance. 'Love is patient' (1 Corinthians 13:4).

> *Be patient, then, brothers and sisters, until the Lord's coming. See how the farmer waits for the land to yield its valuable crop, patiently waiting for the autumn and spring rains. You too, be patient and stand firm, because the Lord's coming is near. Don't grumble*

against one another, brothers and sisters, or you will be judged. The Judge is standing at the door! Brothers and sisters, as an example of patience in the face of suffering, take the prophets who spoke in the name of the Lord. As you know, we count as blessed those who have persevered. You have heard of Job's perseverance and have seen what the Lord finally brought about. The Lord is full of compassion and mercy. (James 5:7-11)

Kindness

This is a meek, gracious, unpretentious and delightful flavour of the fruit of the Spirit. Have we not all been on the receiving end of a kind word, perhaps on many occasions? 'Anxiety weighs down the heart, but a kind word cheers it up' (Proverbs 12:25). Kindness is not transmitted on a downward vertical or inclined plane, i.e. emanating from a person higher up in favour of someone on a lower level; no, it is transmitted and received horizontally, heart to heart, mind to mind. This is why we appreciate the kindness of Jesus so much; he is the Son of Man, he came in order to be on our level.

1 Corinthians 13:4: 'Love is kind.'

2 Corinthians 6:6: 'Kindness in the Holy Spirit.'

Goodness

A verse in Mrs C.F. Alexander's hymn 'There is a green hill far away' reads:

> *He died that we might be forgiven,*
> ***He died to make us good,***

> *That we might go at last to heaven,*
> *Saved by his precious blood.*[62]

There is no other way to become good in God's sight. And there is more, for the Christ who died rose from the dead, ascended into heaven from where, at the Father's bidding, he sent forth the Holy Spirit to, along with much else, ensure that **goodness** emanates, radiates and shines out from his disciples, to bless co-disciples and the world at large. Doubtless God has raised up and equipped a great host of past and present saints who have been and are models of his intent regarding goodness. One in particular springs to mind – Barnabas:

> *He [Barnabas] was a **good** man, full of the Holy Spirit, and faith, and a great number of people were brought to the Lord. (Acts 11:24)*

This man's life offered the fruit of the Spirit, tasting of goodness, to the Christian communities he frequented, to individuals such as Saul of Tarsus and their young helper John Mark, to hosts of people who observed him and listened to his teaching. He was a man of firm conviction who stuck by the principles he had received from God, but he was humble, generous, self-deprecating, sacrificial and motivated by love for God, for those for whom he held a particular measure of responsibility and, noticeably, for those who disagreed with him.

A sharp disagreement arose between Barnabas and Paul; it is documented in Acts 15:36-40. From subsequent Scriptures we learn that the rift between the two apostles was healed.

---

[62]. C.F. Alexander (1848), 'There is a green hill far away', https://hymnary.org/text/there_is_a_green_hill_far_away (accessed 1.4.24).

We are not informed of the details of this healing, but we can be sure that goodness, birthed by the Spirit, played a large part.

Fruit, born of the Spirit and expressed in goodness, can resolve the acutest of disputes to the satisfaction of all sides.

Faithfulness

Under the previous heading we have reflected on the mutual bruising and battering inflicted on the friendship and close collaboration that had existed between two of Christ's servants. Now we can add that although both men were hurt, it is clear that a deep sense of faithfulness to each other remained intact. The healing process probably spanned several years, but it is also likely that their faithfulness to each other continued uninterrupted; doubtless they prayed constantly and fervently for each other, and neither would ever have a bad word to say about the other. They remained faithful. In time this characteristic of the fruit of the Spirit was to bring them into reconciliation, for we are told that John Mark, the young man defended by Barnabas over whom they had disputed, had become a close colleague of Paul (2 Timothy 4:11).

Another well-known history of constancy and faithfulness is that of Jonathan and David. Theirs was a friendship of love; not a homosexual relationship, but nevertheless one of love between two strong men who remained faithful to each other till parted by death. After Jonathan had been killed David lamented, 'I grieve for you, Jonathan my brother; you were very dear to me. Your love for me was wonderful, more wonderful than that of women' (2 Samuel 1:26). It goes without saying that for Jesus' followers, fidelity within marriage is of paramount importance, and the fruit of the Spirit is a powerful aid in this area. 'Let love and faithfulness never leave you; bind them round your neck' (Proverbs 3:3) like a beautiful necklace.

Hebrews chapter 11 is a pantheon of persons renowned for their faith. In addition to having faith these heroes were also faithful in their living; some, it must be said, knew periods of infidelity, but all finished well. In the concept of faithfulness there is a very strong sense of durability, of standing firm through a long period of time. This comes across in John's letter to his friend Gaius who, it would seem, he had not seen for some time: 'It gave me great joy when some believers came and testified about your faithfulness to the truth, telling how you continue to walk in it' (3 John 3).

Gentleness

For most of us this virtue is very feminine; maybe that is so. We imagine that it was very present in the way Mary nursed Jesus as a baby, and then accompanied him through all the phases of childhood, youth and manhood. But this did not prevent her from being very firm, even stern, with her 12-year-old son when she felt that he had acted without due consideration for her and Joseph. In our own experience we may know physically strong and powerful men who are amazingly gentle with small children, the sick and the frail elderly. We do not doubt that Jesus was gentle, meek and mild, for that is what the gospels show him to be; he said, 'I am gentle and humble in heart'

(Matthew 11:29). Nevertheless, the same records tell us how his moral power and strength, perhaps his physical power too, came to the fore when he drove the traders and money lenders out of the temple, when he denounced hypocrites, when he cast out demons and when he spoke authoritatively to the raging sea. Can we not conclude that gentleness is a sign of, and is sourced by, moral strength? And what greater source of inner and spiritual strength is there than the indwelling Holy Spirit, when by this Spirit we are able to give 'a gentle answer [that] turns away wrath, but a harsh word stirs up anger' (Proverbs 15:1).

1 Peter 3:4 speaks of 'the unfading beauty of a gentle and quiet spirit'.

Ephesians 4:2: 'Be completely humble and gentle.'

Philippians 4:5: 'Let your gentleness be evident to all. The Lord is near.'

1 Peter 3:15: 'Always be prepared to give an answer to everyone who asks you to give the reason for the hope that you have. **But do this with gentleness and respect.**'

Self-control

All nine characteristics of the fruit of the Spirit are interdependent, and we have previously noted that it is on the first – love – that the remaining eight are especially dependent. We would now suggest that only in the presence of *self-control* can the first eight find authentic expression. We do not claim to be well developed in this area, and, dear reader, you may feel the same way about yourself. We are still in the beginners' class, and, insofar as progress depends upon us (*self* that is), we shall probably find achieving better things extremely difficult. Consequently, the knowledge that self-control is an element of the fruit of the indwelling Spirit is hugely encouraging and unburdening. This incites us to yield to the Holy Spirit, to open up more and more of our person to him, to listen to his voice (through meditating Scripture, through heeding the example of others, through prophecy, through his speaking directly to our spirit . . .). In our own circle of family and friends there are several persons who have been suffering in their bodies for months or years; they are often in pain, in some cases permanently so, yet they have learnt to live with their pain; some are disabled following strokes and their mobility is either much reduced or almost non-existent, yet they resist depression and continue to shine. This is self-control in particular circumstances, and many are in such situations, including the deprived and the oppressed. For them, and for the rest of us who are not suffering in any particular way, the Spirit leads us, day after day, to stay on the way of the cross, and to become more and more Spirit-controlled.

1 Thessalonians 5:6: 'Let us be awake and sober.' (Also v.8.)

Titus 1:6-8: 'An elder must be . . . self-controlled, upright, holy and disciplined.' (Also, Titus 2:2,5,6,12.)

12

The Ministry Gifts

The ministry gifts we have in mind are those set out in Ephesians 4:11 and 1 Corinthians 12:28-29. Are there other divine appointments, ministry gifts? Very probably! Most of us could readily suggest other functions and vocations which we consider to be ministries given by God to the church and to humanity. This said, with one important exception, we will only comment specifically on the gifts listed in the two passages mentioned, but many of the principles we will endeavour to develop are no doubt applicable to all areas of Christian service and ministry.

Ephesians 4:11 concerns the gifts of apostle, prophet, evangelist, pastor and teacher (alternatively pastor/teacher). The wider passage, verses 7-16, tells us that these gifts are made 'to his people' by the ascended Lord Jesus Christ; it is he 'who ascended higher than all the heavens' who gives these so essential ministers and ministries, the purpose being 'to equip his people for works of service, so that the body of Christ may be built up until we all reach unity in the faith and in the knowledge of the Son of God and become mature, attaining to the whole measure of the fullness of Christ'. The scope here is awesome!

The twelve apostles of the Lamb (Revelation 21:14) and the early church apostles, such as James the Lord's brother, Barnabas, Paul and others (maybe Timothy and Titus, Andronicus and Junia – Romans 16:7), were wonderfully used in pioneering, leading, consolidating, guiding, maintaining doctrinal purity, insisting on integrity in personal and community relations, overseeing, accompanying young Christian communities through persecution and much else. The prophets, such as Agabus, Ananias and Silas, ministered side by side with the apostles, conveying messages of instruction, guidance and prediction received from God. The evangelists, such as Phillip, propagated the good news of salvation to all, Jews and non-Jews, and, in common with the other ministries, were used in healing the sick and bringing liberty to persons in demonic bondage. No doubt they also encouraged the communities and their members to testify freely and communicate the gospel. The local communities were shepherded by elders (that is pastors/teachers) who cared for, instructed and led the believers to spiritual maturity and active Christian service. So it was that the early church grew, expanded and was preserved despite the hostility of political and religious authorities and the people in general.

We note that the pastors, or elders, of local communities served in plurality and not singly. In Acts 20 we have the account of Paul's farewell to the Ephesian elders; he met with them as a group and charged them collectively to 'keep watch over yourselves and all the flock of which the Holy Spirit has made you overseers. Be shepherds of the church of God, which he bought with his own blood' (v.28). No one was singled out as the pastor, for they were all to function pastorally. They could have all been designated 'pastor', but it seems that it was customary to use the term 'elder' for all the local community shepherds. Their strength and safeguard was in their plurality, or collegiality; this was certainly good for each of them and for the Ephesian church. Dear readers, concerning the important matter of local leadership, do you not think that our contemporary churches would do well to look again at the Ephesian example, and also that of Crete (Titus 1:5-9), Pisidia (Acts 14:24), Philippi (Philippians 1:1) and Jerusalem (Acts 15:4)?

The epistle writers seem to use the terms elders, overseers and bishops synonymously and not as indicative of level of seniority. The term pastor (shepherd), when applied to men, appears just once in the New Testament, i.e. Ephesians 4:11. It is a beautifully evocative term that draws our attention to Jesus and to the group of shepherds who, whilst watching over their flocks at night, were visited by an angel and were encompassed by the glory of the Lord. It is good for Christian shepherds to keep watch together!

To the elders among you, I appeal as a fellow elder and a witness of Christ's sufferings who also will share in the glory to be revealed: be shepherds of God's flock that is under your care, watching over them – not because you must, but because you are willing, as God wants you to be; not pursuing dishonest gain, but eager to serve; not lording it over those entrusted to you, but being examples to the flock. (1 Peter 5:1-3)

Peter was an apostle, and there were, and still are, times when an apostle must assert his apostleship, but here the fisherman identified with the elders, the local pastors, and this strikes us as evidence that all concerned were in submission to the Holy Spirit, he who teaches and brings about Christ-like character. Are not the designations 'pastor' (Ephesians 4:11), and 'elder, overseer', widely used in Acts and the Letters, synonymous? They certainly do not have hierarchic significance.

The 1 Corinthians 12:28-30 passage includes other appointments in addition to those of apostle, prophet and teacher, each of which also figures in Ephesians 4:11 (NIV 1984); the additions are 'workers of miracles', those having 'gifts of healing', those able to 'help others' (simply 'helps' in the KJV), those with 'gifts of administration' and those 'speaking in other kinds of tongues'. It would seem that we should understand these further works and gifts as ministries in the same measure that we do the appointments to minister as apostle, prophet and teacher. Miracles, healings, helping out in every imaginable way, efficient administration and glossolalia in the early church were certainly integral and essential to the warp and the weft of Christian community life, as they should be today, and certainly are in many places throughout the world. In 1 Corinthians the possession and exercise of spiritual gifts are very much to the fore, and this implies that holiness has to be the principal characteristic of the ministries concerned; Jesus and the **Holy** Spirit promote holiness in the exercise of the gifts they bestow.

The most important ministry!

Is there a ministry which is more important than all the others? We believe that there is, and it is the exception to which we alluded earlier, for it is not included in the Ephesian and Corinthian texts. We have in mind that all-inclusive ministry in which all Christians share, **the priesthood of all believers**. This Bible truth is one of the three vital, hitherto neglected, doctrines that the Reformation brought to light. The apostle Peter wrote about this ministry in his letter to Christians in Asia Minor:

> *As you come to him [Jesus], the living Stone – rejected by humans but chosen by God and precious to him – you also, like living stones, are being built into a spiritual house to be a **holy priesthood**, offering spiritual sacrifices acceptable to God through Jesus Christ . . . But you are a chosen people, **a royal priesthood**, a holy nation, God's special possession, that you may declare the praises of him who called you out of darkness into his wonderful light. Once you were not a people, but now you are the people of God; once you had not received mercy, but now you have received mercy. (1 Peter 2:4-5, 9-10)*

By virtue of the New Birth, that is, as Jesus explained to Nicodemus, by being born of the Spirit and the Word, every repentant, now regenerated, sinner becomes a priest, a holy and royal priest! Taken as a whole this holy and regal company is God's house, his people, his **priesthood**, whose primary duty and pleasure is to offer spiritual sacrifices and praises to God.

In similar style to Peter the apostle John, writing from Patmos to the seven churches of Asia Minor (Revelation

1:5-6) writes of 'him who loves us and has freed us from our sins by his blood, and has made us to be a **kingdom and priests to serve his God and Father** – to him be glory and power for ever and ever! Amen.' Further on in Revelation (5:9-10; 20:6) we learn more about the very wide scope, geographical coverage and duration of this priesthood. Christians today should be aware of being participants in this ministry, realising that this is our most vital service, the ministry we all share, the ministry which is a cover for, and which authenticates, every specific form of service rendered to Jesus and the Kingdom. It is evident that the participants in this ministry are all on the same plane, equal in all respects. There is no clergy-laity division, no grading within the priesthood and just one head or chief: 'We have a great high priest who has ascended into heaven, Jesus the Son of God' (Hebrews 4:14). All the 'priests' have privileges and responsibilities, and all are answerable for their stewardship to the 'great high priest'. All need the enablement, the training, the power and the wisdom of the Holy Spirit in order to minister effectively, in harmony with other 'priests' and for fulfilling other specific ministries entrusted to them (e.g. elder, evangelist, administrator, speaker in tongues), in a manner approved by Jesus, the head of the church.

The priesthood of all believers is not uniquely a New Testament truth, for it was God's preference for Israel too in Moses' day (see Exodus 19:6); but the people were unwilling to accept nationwide priesthood and refused YAWH's proposal (Exodus 20:19-21). In response the Lord God put in place for Israel a provisional arrangement with a selective priesthood at its core. Through Moses he appointed Aaron and his sons and their descendants as the only members of this priesthood. He also gave detailed instructions concerning the preparation and qualification of these persons for their priestly vocation and functions. Furthermore, the Lord God spelt out the duties and functions of the Selective Priesthood.

We suggest that Christians today can discover much material to guide them regarding participation in the universal priesthood of the New Covenant (NC) in the clear, strict and demanding principles the Lord God gave to Moses concerning the selective priesthood. These directives are set out in Exodus 29:

Verse 4: 'Bring Aaron and his sons to the entrance to the tent of meeting.' The only candidates were members of the divinely designated family. This principle also applies to the NC priesthood. The designated family members are persons 'born of water and the Spirit' (John 3:5). These regenerated folks are those who have 'received the Spirit of sonship. And by him . . . cry, "Abba, Father." The Spirit himself testifies with our spirit that we are God's children' (Romans 8:15-16 NIV 1984, see also John 1:11-13). At the entrance to the Tent Aaron and his sons were washed 'with water'. So it is for the NC priests; Ephesians 5:26 tells us that Christ washes and purifies his church, 'cleansing her by the washing with water through the word'.

Verses 5-6: 'Take the garments and dress Aaron with the tunic, the robe of the ephod, the ephod itself and the breastpiece. Fasten the ephod on him by its skilfully woven waistband. Put the turban on his head and attach the sacred emblem to the turban.' Priests had to be correctly clothed, including appropriate head covering. Each item certainly conveys figurative significance worthy of consideration, which readers may wish to research. Our purpose is simply to acknowledge our need, as NC priests, of the only acceptable clothing, that is the person of Jesus and his attributes. 'You who were baptised into Christ have clothed yourselves with Christ' (Galatians 3:27) tells us that NC priests are persons who have been baptised into Christ and 'have clothed [themselves] with Christ'. Those to whom we minister must see Jesus, his wisdom, righteousness, holiness and redeeming grace (1 Corinthians 1:30). Only the Holy Spirit can bring this about.

Verse 7: 'Take the anointing oil and anoint him [Aaron] by pouring it on his head.' Psalm 133 tells us in graphic terms that an abundant amount of oil was poured on Aaron's head! The sacred and precious anointing oil, symbol of the Holy Spirit, authenticated the Aaronic priesthood and assured its continuation for generations to come (see Exodus 40:14-15). The existence and the functioning of the NC priesthood is totally reliant on the person and work of the Holy Spirit; he regenerates the repentant, by him the new born are baptised into (placed in) the body of Christ, the church. It is in him that Jesus baptises believers with an anointing of power, he sanctifies and it is he who equips the NC priesthood for carrying out the multiple aspects of its ministry. 'Now it is God who makes both us and you stand firm in Christ. He anointed us, set his seal of ownership on us, and put his Spirit in our hearts' (2 Corinthians 1:21-22, see also 1 John 2:21-27). The public ministry of Jesus, our Great High Priest, began only after he had received the anointing of the Spirit (the Spirit descended upon him in the form of a dove just after John the Baptist baptised him in the river Jordan); a short while later our High Priest declared, 'The Spirit of the Lord is on me, because he has anointed me to preach good news to the poor . . .' (Luke 4:18).

Verses 19-21: these verses show us that those chosen for the priesthood must be associated with sacrificially shed blood:

> *Take the other ram, and Aaron and his sons shall lay their hands on its head. Slaughter it, take some of its blood and put it on the lobes of the right ears of Aaron and his sons, on the thumbs of their right hands, and on the big toes of their right feet. Then splash blood against the sides of the altar. And take some of the blood on the altar and some of the anointing oil and sprinkle it on Aaron and his garments and on his sons and their garments. Then he and his sons and their garments will be consecrated.*

Participants in the universal priesthood need to be continually associated with the shed blood of Christ, the Lamb of God, for he is both Great High Priest and sacrifice:

- For forgiveness: 'In him we have redemption through his blood, the forgiveness of sins, in accordance with the riches of God's grace' (Ephesians 1:7).
- For frequent cleansing: 'If we walk in the light, as he is in the light . . . the blood of Jesus, his Son, purifies us from all sin' (1 John 1:7).
- For presence: 'Now in Christ Jesus you who once were far away have been brought near by the blood of Christ' (Ephesians 2:13, see also Hebrews 10:19-20).
- In order to receive authority and power to minister; L.E. Jones wrote:

> *Would you do service for Jesus your King?*
> *There's power in the blood, power in the blood;*
> *Would you live daily his praises to sing?*
> *There's wonderful power in the blood.*[63]

Having seen how God's instructions concerning the designation and consecration of the Mosaic priests enlighten us regarding the inclusion of today's believers in, and equipment for, the NC priesthood, we should also take note of the duties and functions of Aaron and his sons, for these can model our understanding of the ministry which should be exercised by the universal priesthood.

Shortly before his death Moses commended and blessed Israel's tribes. Of Levi he said:

> *He watched over your **word** and guarded your **covenant**. He teaches your **precepts** to Jacob and your law to Israel. He offers **incense** before you and whole burnt **offerings** on your altar. **Bless** all his skills, Lord, and **be pleased** with the work of his hands. (Deuteronomy 33:9-11).*

This commendation and prayer for the Old Testament priesthood enshrines principles that are fundamental to the NC priesthood:

Heeding God's **word** and putting it into **practice** (James 1:16-27): 'He [the Father] chose to give us birth through the **word of truth**, that we might be a kind of firstfruits of all he created' (v.18); 'Do not merely listen to the word, and so deceive yourselves. Do what it says' (v.22).

---

63. L.E. Jones (1899), 'There is Power in the Blood', https://hymnary.org/text/would_you_be_free_from_the_burden_jones (accessed 2.4.24).

Faithfulness to the **New Covenant** inaugurated by Jesus: good and transparent **relationship** with God and fellow priests is a key element in the NC, and calls for constant 'guarding'; we belong to the Lord and to each other (see Deuteronomy 7:6). Concerning the Lord's Supper, the fellowship or good relationship meal, we read, 'Everyone ought to examine themselves before they eat of the bread and drink from the cup' (1 Corinthians 11:28).

Teaching God's precepts: as priests we all teach, often well, sometimes badly, by our acts, our attitudes, our example and our words. NC priests are 'letter[s] . . . known and read by everyone. You show that you are a letter from Christ . . . written not with ink but with the **Spirit** of the living God, not on tablets of stone but on tablets of human hearts' (2 Corinthians 3:2-4).

Prayerful living is the priesthood's lifestyle: intercessory and worshipful prayer; unceasing and ascending, just like the Old Testament incense. 'Be joyful always; pray continually; give thanks in all circumstances, for this is God's will for you in Christ Jesus' (1 Thessalonians 5:16-18 NIV 1984).

Sacrifices and offerings should be complete and **total**; way beyond our capacity we would all say, but this is what the NC Scriptures require. 1 Peter 2:5 says that we are to offer '**spiritual sacrifices** acceptable to God through Jesus Christ'. What a comfort it is to know that our offerings, so often partial and tinged by self-interest, go to the Father via the Son, who purifies them before passing them on. This reality helps us when seeking to heed Romans 12:1 where we are called 'to offer [our] bodies as a **living sacrifice**, holy and pleasing to God – this [being] your true and proper worship'. Hebrews 13:15-16 speaks of praise, doing good and sharing as sacrifices which NC priests should offer to God.

The Aaronic priests fulfilled other duties and ministries: blessing the people, by means of this well known and still much appreciated text:

> *The LORD bless you and keep you; the LORD make his face shine on you and be gracious to you; the LORD turn his face towards you and give you peace. (Numbers 6:23-27)*

'To bless' was, and remains, far more than a concerned wish regarding someone's welfare. The priest pronounced the blessing in the form of a prayer, and consequently it was endued with authority and power. The person who blesses is a canal through whom the blessing is transmitted. We, of the NC priesthood, are even called on to 'Bless those who persecute you' (Romans 12:14), and that is being done today by many Christians. This is an area which necessitates particular dependence on the Holy Spirit.

The identification of certain illnesses, such as leprosy, supervision of their treatment, verification treatment and offering sacrifices on behalf of the healed (see Leviticus 13 and 14). Christians today are equipped to discern the nature and cause of ills suffered by persons, communities and humanity globally, to communicate the remedies and treatments that the Lord God has made available, to accompany those who ask for further guidance and to gladly minister to those who accept God's way for them. There are many facets to ministry in this area, one being the 'ministry of reconciliation' of which Paul and Timothy write in 2 Corinthians 5:11-21. In recent years, and still today, the people of Northern Ireland, Ruanda, Burundi and South Africa have, in some measure, experienced this ministry, in which local Christians, members of the universal priesthood, have very actively participated.

The Bible relates other instances of priesthood ministry at national level; one is that of Ezra the priest who returned to Jerusalem from exile to find that immorality, discouragement, neglect of God's ordinances and unfaithfulness regarding his precepts concerning relationships with other peoples were rife amongst the people of Israel. Ezra called everyone to order, to abandon their evil ways and return to the Lord, which they did; nationwide restoration brought about renewal of nationhood and the completion of the rebuilding of Jerusalem. For the full story read from Ezra 7 through Nehemiah. We might ask . . . what does God want the NC priesthood to do in our respective countries in the face of widespread moral and spiritual decline?

In all of these spheres of priestly activity there is need for the gifts of the Holy Spirit (1 Corinthians 14:7-11), the fruit of the Spirit (Galatians 5:22-23) and the graces which flow to believers from Jesus Christ (2 Peter 1:3-9), and through them to others.

By and large the Old Testament priesthood's duties and functions were routine, regular and concentrated in and around the tabernacle or temple, but they had to be ready for the unexpected, the unusual, the big challenge. Three of these challenges were the key roles God gave them when: (i) all Israel crossed the Jordan (Joshua 3:14-17); (ii) Jericho was taken (Joshua 6:1-5); and (iii) Jehoshaphat conquered the Moabites and the Ammonites (2 Chronicles

20:18-22). The New Covenant priesthood is also involved in combat and conquest, not just occasionally but daily; its arms are spiritual:

Be strong in the Lord and in his mighty power. Put on the full armour of God, so that you can take your stand against the devil's schemes. For our struggle is not against flesh and blood, but against the rulers, against the authorities, against the powers of this dark world and against the spiritual forces of evil in the heavenly realms. (Ephesians 6:10-12)

The weapons we fight with are not the weapons of the world. On the contrary, they have divine power to demolish strongholds. (2 Corinthians 10:4)

With the Holy Spirit we receive power to conquer! In the face of hostility and brutality the Christians of the early centuries of our era were pacific, non-violent in their response, and history tells how this was beneficial for the church and humanity.

E.C.W. Boulton has left us, we of the contemporary New Covenant priesthood, these lines to say or sing together:

Called to separation with the crucified,
Temples of the Spirit, saved and sanctified,
Set apart for service, by God's hand ordained,
We the cross have taken, by his love constrained.

Christ the veil has entered, with the blood he shed,
Sin's great debt is cancelled, love's own feast is spread;
Now in Christ we're chosen kings and priests to be,
Living offerings bringing, his own blood our plea.

Step by step with Jesus,
All along life's way,
Now the cross and conflict,
Then the perfect day.[64]

---

64. E.C.W. Boulton, 'Called to separation', *Redemption Hymnal* (1955), hymn 602.

13

Blasphemy, Grieving, Resisting or Pleasing the Holy Spirit

Blasphemy

The principal text we need to read and seek to understand is Matthew 12:31-32, which reports Jesus as saying:

> And so I tell you, every kind of sin and slander can be forgiven, but blasphemy against the Spirit will not be forgiven. Anyone who speaks a word against the Son of Man will be forgiven, but anyone who speaks against the Holy Spirit will not be forgiven, either in this age or in the age to come.

The parallel account in Mark 3:28-29 is not so full, but its ending rams home the awfulness of the condemnation:

> Truly I tell you, people can be forgiven all their sins and every slander they utter, but whoever blasphemes against the Holy Spirit will never be forgiven; they are guilty of an eternal sin.

Mark adds, 'He said this because **they were saying**, "He has an impure spirit"' (v.30).

Unsurprisingly commentators concur in suggesting that the key to acquiring a measure of understanding of the nature of blasphemy against the Holy Spirit is the context in which the Master spoke. It seems that it was a Sabbath day; Jesus had already taught and healed a number of sick persons when:

> *They brought to him a demon-possessed man who was blind and mute, and Jesus healed him, so that he could both talk and see. All the people were astonished and said, 'Could this be the Son of David?' But when the Pharisees heard this, they said, 'It is only by Beelzebub, the prince of demons, that this fellow drives out demons.' (Matthew 12:22-24)*

Jesus knew what the Pharisees were thinking (and murmuring amongst themselves it would seem), and he roundly reproved them, concluding with, 'If it is by the Spirit of God that I drive out demons, then the kingdom of God has come upon you' (v.28). Moments later Jesus issued the denunciation cited above.

Adam Clarke considers that blasphemy against the Holy Spirit occurs:

> *When the person obstinately attributed those works to the devil, which he had the fullest evidence could be wrought only by the Spirit of God. That this, and nothing else, is the sin against the Holy Spirit, is evident from the connection in this place, and more particularly from Mark 3:28-30. 'All sins shall be forgiven unto*

the sons of men, and blasphemies wherewith soever they shall blaspheme; but he that shall blaspheme against the Holy Ghost hath never forgiveness, but is in danger of eternal damnation; Because they said, He hath an unclean spirit.' Here the matter is made clear beyond the smallest doubt – the unpardonable sin, as some term it, is neither less nor more than ascribing the miracles Christ wrought, by the power of God, to the spirit of the devil. Many sincere people have been grievously troubled with apprehensions that they had committed the unpardonable sin; but let it be observed that no man who believes the Divine mission of Jesus Christ, ever can commit this sin.[65]

This matter is weighty; the consequences, if found guilty of committing this sin, are grave and beyond our ability to fully grasp. Let us therefore hold fast to and proclaim all that the Holy Spirit has done and continues to do through Jesus the Son.

Saul of Tarsus was a blasphemer, but not against the Holy Spirit, and he obtained mercy. In his first letter to Timothy (1:13) he writes, 'Even though I was once a blasphemer and a persecutor and a violent man, I was shown mercy because I acted in ignorance and unbelief.'

Grieving

Very probably all adult human beings are very conscious of having grieved another, a loved one or someone who has held us in esteem, to whom we have occasioned

---

65. Adam Clarke, *Commentary on Matthew* (Pokeno, NZ: Titus Books, 2013), Kindle Edition, locations 3950-3960.

great distress by our unkind acts, or thoughtless words. We, maybe you too, cannot forget some of our deeds and words which have deeply hurt someone who loved and/or trusted us; maybe we have been forgiven, but we cannot forget our thoughtlessness. Grieving can occur between Christians, within Christian families and Christian communities.

Scripture makes clear that Christians, individually and collectively, can grieve God. Our present concern is the possibility of grieving the Holy Spirit.

In Ephesians 4:17-31 Paul forthrightly mentions a number of behavioural characteristics which should not be present in a Christian's life. Paul insists that his readers must no longer live as Gentiles do, or allow their hearts to become hardened, or lose all sensitivity, or give themselves over to sensuality, or indulge in impurity and lust, putting off falsehood and untruthfulness, not allowing the devil to get a foothold in their lives, not to steal, to be industrious, avoiding unwholesome talk, banishing all bitterness, rage and anger, brawling and slander, along with every form of malice. Against the sombre background of these detailed warnings and exhortations the appeal in verse 30 to the Ephesians and to us with force, clarity and compassion, 'Do not grieve the Holy Spirit of God, with whom you were sealed for the day of redemption.'

God the Holy Spirit loves us, and he invites us to allow him to show us in what ways we are grieving him. He will search our hearts and minds, convict us of sin, call us to repentance and make the sin-cleansing blood of Jesus available to us. We are in a relationship of love with the Holy Spirit and with our fellow Christians. Love grieved is a sad and painful picture. Let us then 'be kind and compassionate to one another, forgiving each other, just as in Christ God forgave [us]' (v.32).

What should we do when we become conscious of having grieved the Holy Spirit? King David, he who had committed adultery followed by murder by proxy, subsequently became deeply aware of the awfulness of his transgressions, of having grieved God. In Psalm 51:10-12, in profound distress he cries out, 'Create in me a pure heart, O God, and renew a steadfast spirit within me. Do not . . . take your Holy Spirit from me. Restore to me the joy of your salvation and grant me a willing spirit, to sustain me.'

No doubt the grieving we occasion the Spirit is often collective, i.e. we and our local church, or denomination, or outreach team, or, or . . .! Collective repentance is necessary, followed by reparation and/or reconciliation. It seems probable that, through the long history of the church, many periods of spiritual awakening have been birthed when Christian communities have sought pardon for having grieved the Lord. A well-known case was that of the Moravians at Herrnhut (see our chapter 7 on 'Circumcision of the Heart by the Spirit'). In the gospels the Holy Spirit is likened to a sensitive dove who seeks constantly to strengthen Christians in their relationships with each other and with their Lord. In contrast much in human nature and conduct is offensive, distressing and grievous to the Spirit and to our fellow believers. Vertical and horizontal relationships can be hurt, sometimes grievously so. Thankfully, when we allow the Spirit to correct us and rectify the wrongs in our lives, we can bring him great pleasure, great joy.

Resisting

Acts chapters 6 and 7 tell the heart-rending account to the appointment of seven of the male disciples, one being Stephen, to look after the needs of certain widows. Stephen, a man full of God's grace and power, did great wonders and miraculous signs among the people. This aroused fierce opposition to what Stephen said and did. Stephen warned then of the grave situation they had put themselves in saying, 'You stiff-necked people! Your hearts and ears are still uncircumcised. You are just like your ancestors: you always **resist** the Holy Spirit!' (Acts 7:51). These people then dragged Stephen out of the city – and stoned him! Clearly, resistance to the Spirit carries heavy penalties for the guilty, and suffering for the innocent.

Pleasing

The story of the friendship and common purpose that Barnabas and Saul, also called Paul, enjoyed is related in Acts chapters 9 – 15. Their relationship was solid, built upon mutual trust and appreciation of each other's gifts, strengths and capacities. They stood together when Saul was initially distrusted by most of the disciples at Jerusalem, when working and teaching together at Antioch, when with a small team they left Antioch to tell the good news in Cyprus, Asia Minor and Syria, when they subsequently met with the Council at Jerusalem to discuss the Gentile question, when, with other delegates, they returned to Antioch to deliver the Council's recommendations, when for a while afterwards they 'remained in Antioch, where they and many others taught and preached the word of the Lord' (Acts 15:35-36) and, finally, when together they decided to return to the places where they had preached the word to see how the brethren were doing. All this paints a delightful picture of harmony, shared convictions and purposeful fraternity, but this idyllic picture was suddenly and surprisingly spoilt. The two men, such close friends, sharply disagreed on whether or not John Mark should accompany them, so they separated. As to who was right, who was wrong, or whether both were in some way right and/or wrong, is not our concern here. We must simply assume that the Holy Spirit was grieved, displeased by their inability to discern his directions. Each went his separate way.

Happily, the story does not end there. The Holy Spirit is so patient, persevering and communicative. It seems to have taken years for the rift to be closed, for the dissension to be healed, for the grieving to give way to pleasure, but Scripture indicates that over time Paul came to fully appreciate John Mark, and harmony, respect and brotherly love were restored between the two apostles (2 Timothy 4:11). How happy and pleased the Spirit must have been.

Who amongst us never had a sharp disagreement with a colleague and friend? Sometimes the dissension has seemed to be justified, but oft times it was not. We remember the grieving occasioned to our friend; he was hurt. We also realised, perhaps not straight away, that the Holy Spirit's grief was even more acute. Oh, what pleasure we and our friend knew when reconciliation occurred. We are, of course, unable to measure the degree of pleasure the grieved Spirit knows when dissension between Christians is put aside and unity restored.

In Galatians 6 we read of a much simpler, down to earth, way of pleasing the Holy Spirit; it is by doing good, whenever we have the opportunity, 'to all people, especially to those who belong to the family of believers' (see 6:10). Prior to this counsel Paul reminded his readers that, throughout life, Christians have choices to make with regard to what they sow. They can either sow to please their sinful nature, and from that nature reap destruction, or they can sow to please the Spirit, and from the Spirit reap eternal life (6:7-9). Verse 9 advises, 'Let us not become weary in doing good, for at the proper time we will reap a harvest if we do not give up.' Maybe we can all think of folk who in practical and spiritual ways have spent a lifetime heeding this advice, and, as a consequence, enjoy contentment, peace and happiness in their communion with the Lord and his people, possibly despite being misunderstood!

14

Suffering

Christians are accustomed to associating Jesus, God the Son, with suffering and sufferers, also God the Father but much less so God the Holy Spirit.

Initially Jesus' conception occasioned much heartache and suffering to Joseph, probably to Mary too. The circumstances of his birth were a mix of rejoicing and suffering. King Herod's slaughtering of all boys two years old and under in Bethlehem and its vicinity brought immense suffering to many parents and their families. There followed a period of forced exile during which, we can assume, neither the young lad nor his parents had a comfortable time. The return to Nazareth may have eased the pressure on the family, which grew with the arrival of brothers and sisters for the eldest son. But years later, prior to his death and resurrection, Jesus' siblings made known their disbelief in him as the Christ, the Messiah, and that certainly hurt him.

Progressively, throughout the period of his public ministry Jesus' suffering included rejection, exclusion, unbelief, shunning, bearing the burdens of his disciples and the crowds, physical and moral hardship, betrayal, condemnation, crucifixion, being forsaken by his Father, being a sacrificial Lamb and dying in indescribable physical and spiritual pain. Who can comprehend and describe his passion, his suffering? Thankfully the Scriptures come to our aid. From Genesis to Revelation Jesus' suffering is described and explained:

- Genesis 3:15: 'He [the Christ] will crush your head, and you [Satan] will strike his heel.'
- Isaiah 53: with its many predictions of Messiah's sufferings.
- Matthew 16:21: Jesus explains to his disciples 'that he must go up to Jerusalem and suffer many things at the hands of the elders, the chief priests and the teachers of the law, and that he must be killed.'
- The several accounts of Jesus' crucifixion. A summary statement in 1 Peter 4:1: 'Christ suffered in his body.'
- Revelation 5:12: 'Worthy is the Lamb, who was slain.' Paul wanted to know Christ in every way possible this side of heaven, including by way of 'participation in his sufferings, becoming like him in his death' (Philippians 3:10). Christians are greatly strengthened and comforted by the knowledge that their Lord is very much a partaker in whatever suffering they may endure.

The Son suffers, and so does the Father. Jesus' illuminating story, recorded in Luke 15, concerning a father who had two sons, both of whom, in very different ways, occasioned him heart-breaking suffering, clearly illustrates how much God the Father is hurt by the selfish behaviour of human kind to whom he gave life. The Bible relates how the Father effected many measures of reconciliation (for example the introduction during the Old Testament period of several covenants, and the sending of a succession of prophetic messengers), but Israel and humanity in general failed to repent and cooperate. The suffering Father then undertook to suffer even more; he sent his Son, his only Son, to be a sacrificial Lamb.

That God the Father and God the Son suffer is clearly portrayed in Scripture. That God the Holy Spirit also suffers may not be so evident from the reading of the texts, but given that 'the LORD our God, the LORD is one' (Deuteronomy 6:4), it follows that the three Persons of the Trinity share the same attributes: each is eternal, each is love, each suffers. When the Son suffered on the cross, the Father and the Son suffered with him, and so did the Holy Spirit. There is no division in the Trinity.

Now let us briefly consider a few of the forms of suffering the Holy Spirit probably experiences, and how he comes to our aid when we suffer in similar ways.

The suffering of rejection and/or exclusion. The Holy Spirit had breathed life into Adam, our common ancestor. Thereafter he and Eve enjoyed sweet communion with God their Creator, until the day when they rejected the guidance and fellowship of the Spirit. They hardened their hearts to what the Spirit was saying to their consciences, and sin, exclusion from the garden and separation from God (spiritual death) became their lot. They had wilfully rejected the Lordship of the Holy Spirit and excluded him from their lives, with the result that they themselves, and all mankind with them, came to know exclusion from the Kingdom. We cannot grasp the immensity of the suffering that this brought to the Holy Spirit, but readers may find it in the line of thought we have tried to develop in the third chapter ('Dove') of book 1 of this trilogy,[66] an approach which helps our understanding of the sensitivity and suffering of the Spirit. In Psalm 55 David writes of a dove, in suffering, who, feeling rejected and homeless, seeks refuge in the wilderness. When we, the church of Jesus, wherever we may be in the world, are in such a situation we are succoured, comforted and strengthened by the Holy Spirit.

The suffering of unbelief or disbelief. Jesus drove out demons by the Spirit of God (Matthew 12:22-28). But many on-lookers were unbelieving. Through the centuries of gospel propagation which have been blessed by multitudes of new births, revivals, renewals, miracles, community transformations, much praise and worship and the progressive building of Christ's body, the church, unbelief regarding the person and work of the Holy Spirit has often been present, even, it would seem, in Christian hearts. Will this also be the picture when, in the last of the last days, God pours out his Spirit on all mankind? Today, in many places sincere Christians seek to share their convictions and their experiences regarding the Holy Spirit with other equally sincere Christians but are not always believed. This occasions suffering, often on all sides. Open-hearted discussion, a willingness to engage in Scripture-based re-examination of one's position (or the stance of one's denomination) should be undertaken, but suffering

---

66. Michael E.J. Wright, *Biblical Metaphors for the Holy Spirit* (Malcolm Down Publishing, 2023), pp.47-64.

there often is, and all should be open to the enlightenment of the Holy Spirit, for it is he who always suffers most. Misunderstanding of Scripture, or of the doctrinal/experiential position of other Christians, is sometimes the cause of the suffering occasioned by disbelief. Christians who show their enthusiasm for the workings of the Holy Spirit and manifestations of his power (particularly in the operation of spiritual gifts) are sometimes shunned by other Christians, and, we must add, vice versa. How should we seek to make progress together? Readers probably feel, as we do, that the only way to maintain and augment harmony between ourselves and other Christians who hold to other positions is to constantly heed Ephesians 4:3, 'Make every effort to keep the unity of the Spirit through the bond of peace', coupled with a longing that the nine characteristics of the fruit of the Spirit be produced in us and our community.

The suffering of spurned love. Spurned love is surely one of the severest pains a human being can have to endure, and the suffering may be lifelong. In this connection we immediately think of the spurned love of a lover, a fiancé(e) or a spouse, but a child's love can be spurned by its parents or its friends, a parent's love can be spurned, a friend's too, and so on. The suffering is deep and often incomprehensible. When we, who have been the objects of the Spirit's care, comfort, guidance, empowering and love, turn our backs on him, refuse his gifts and spurn his love, we occasion great suffering. Again, the sorrowful cooing, or mourning, of the dove comes to mind. Happily, the way of the cross brings us back to the Dove and reparation of our relationship with him. Furthermore, the suffering Spirit comes to our aid when we become aware of having spurned the love of someone; the pathway of reconciliation is not easy: confession, request of pardon, humbling are necessary.

The suffering of persecution. Persecution is the common lot of probably the greater part of humanity. Certainly, in some measure, all Christians wherever they live, of whatever ethnic group they are a part, suffer persecution. In many countries the degree of suffering is mild, in others hard to bear and in some intense and life threatening. We are indebted to organisations such as Open Doors, The Voice of the Martyrs and Amnesty International for the information, calls to prayer and other means of action that they address to us on behalf of the persecuted. They also endeavour to take practical help to the sufferers. We can also be assured that God the Holy Spirit is very present with the persecuted.

We are all too well aware of many other forms of suffering; much has been written and said on the subject. The Bible contains a wealth of suffering-related teaching and assistance, e.g. many of the psalms, the books of Job, Lamentations, Acts, 1 Peter (4:12-19), 2 Corinthians (4:7-12 and 11:23-33 Paul's testimony).

Whatever suffering we, or the worldwide church, have to bear, the Holy Spirit will always come, in many ways, to comfort us. Probably the most precious of these varied ways is beautifully stated in John's gospel: 'When the Comforter is come . . . he shall testify of me' (15:26 KJV); 'When he, the Spirit of truth, is come, he will guide you into all truth: for he shall not speak of himself; but whatsoever he shall hear, that shall he speak; and he will show you things to come. He shall glorify me: for he shall receive of mine, and shall show it unto you' (16:13-14 KJV).

Sufferers can know no help better than this: to learn more about Jesus, to hear his words, to see him more clearly, to listen to God the Holy Spirit's testimony concerning God the Son.

15

The Blood

A hymn written by Charles Wesley expresses, with simple words, the harmony and oneness that links the Holy Spirit and his role with the blood of Jesus. The first verse reads:

> *Spirit of faith, come down,*
> *Reveal the things of God;*
> *And make to us the Godhead known,*
> *And witness with the blood.*[67]

These lines were probably inspired by 1 John 5:6-8:

This is the one who came by water and blood – Jesus Christ. He did not come by water only, but by water and blood. And it is the Spirit who testifies, because the Spirit is the truth. For there are three that testify: the Spirit, the water and the blood; and the three are in agreement.

Many understand that 'the water' in question is the water of Jesus' baptism, by which he (although sinless) identified

---
67. Charles Wesley (1746), 'Spirit of faith, come down', https://hymnary.org/text/spirit_of_faith_come_down (accessed 18.10.24).

himself with sinful humanity. Others consider 'water' in the context to be a metaphor for the word, God's word. Concerning 'the Spirit' and 'the blood' the only possible understanding is that the Spirit is the Holy Spirit, and the blood is the blood of Jesus, the blood he shed when he was crucified. John tells us that all three – Spirit, water and blood – testify of Jesus, his person and his works. The three combine in unison to attest the deity of Jesus, that he alone is Saviour, Lord and coming King; he is the way, the truth and the life; by none other but he can sinful human beings come to the Father. Furthermore, they act together to assure repentant and believing hearts that they are indeed born of God, are truly disciples of Jesus and are co-heirs with him of the Kingdom. Together they intervene to banish the niggling doubts that seek to disturb the assurance which is the birthright of every Christian, and to thereby enable the believer to live and serve in the liberty and freedom of a son/daughter relationship with God.

The particular emphasis of this chapter is the biblical association of (or agreement between) the Holy Spirit and the blood of Jesus. How are we to assimilate and benefit from this very important teaching? No doubt a number of approaches are equally valid; ours is to set down the following truths concerning Jesus' blood, quoting appropriate texts and suggesting that readers pause over each one (or come back to from time to time, when a particular need is felt), inviting the Holy Spirit to testify appropriately to our heart.

The shed blood of Jesus is:
The blood of atonement
Romans 3:25: 'God presented Christ as a sacrifice of atonement, through the shedding of his blood – to be received by faith.' *Atonement* speaks of a sacrifice that satisfies (appeases) the righteous wrath of God. This is appropriated by faith in Jesus' sacrifice, his shed blood.

The blood of justification
Romans 5:9: 'Since we have been justified by his blood, how much more shall we be saved from God's wrath through him!' *Justification* signifies 'declared righteous'.

The blood of redemption
Ephesians 1:7-8: 'In him [Jesus Christ] we have redemption through his blood, the forgiveness of sins, in accordance with the riches of God's grace that he lavished on us. With all wisdom and understanding.' Slaves (sinners too) find freedom (*redemption*) when a required ransom is paid. (See also Hebrews 9:12.)

The blood of rapprochement
Ephesians 2:13: 'Now in Christ Jesus you who once were far away have been brought near by the blood of Christ', i.e. no longer separate, excluded, foreigners, without hope and without God in the world (see v.12).

The blood that makes peace
Colossians 1:19-20: 'God was pleased . . . through him to reconcile to himself all things, whether things on earth

or things in heaven, by making peace through his blood, shed on the cross.' By the blood of Jesus God replaces by peace the enmity that exists naturally between us and him, between us and our fellows.

> *Peace, perfect peace, in this dark world of sin?*
> *The blood of Jesus whispers peace within.*[68]

The blood of the new covenant

Hebrews 12:22-24: 'You have come . . . to Jesus the mediator of a new covenant, and to the sprinkled blood that speaks a better word than the blood of Abel.' The shed blood of Jesus ratified the new covenant he inaugurated, and it is to that we have come; the covenant between God and the redeemed is secured by the blood and is so attested by the Holy Spirit.

The blood that affords access

It was by virtue of his own blood that Jesus 'entered the Most Holy Place [heaven]' (Hebrews 9:12). It is also by the efficacy of the blood that believers enter into the presence of God.

The blood of continual cleansing

1 John 1:7: 'If we walk in the light, as he [God] is in the light, we have fellowship with one another, and the blood of Jesus, his Son, purifies us from all sin.' The Holy Spirit constrains us to never claim that we have not sinned, but to

---

68. Edward Henry Bickersteth (1875), 'Peace, perfect peace, in this dark world of sin', https://hymnary.org/text/peace_perfect_peace_in_this_dark_world_o (accessed 3.4.24).

constantly ask for cleansing in the blood and to endeavour to walk in the light of God and his word.

The blood empowers for service

Revelation 1:5-6: 'To him who loves us and has **freed us from our sins by his blood**, and has made us to be a kingdom and priests **to serve his God and Father** – to him be glory and power for ever and ever! Amen.'

Hebrews 9:14: 'How much more, then, will the blood of Christ, who through the eternal Spirit offered himself unblemished to God, cleanse our consciences from acts that lead to death, so that we may serve the living God!'

The Spirit witnesses to us that we are cleansed by the blood to serve.

Further lines from Charles Wesley, this time from his hymn 'Arise, my soul, arise':

> *The Father hears him pray,*
> *His dear Anointed One;*
> *He cannot turn away*
> *The presence of his Son,*
> *His Spirit answers to the blood,*
> *And tells me I am born of God.*[69]

---

69. Charles Wesley (1742), 'Arise, my soul, arise', https://hymnary.org/text/arise_my_soul_arise_shake_off_thy_guilty (accessed 3.4.24).

16

The Centrality of Jesus

'Jesus, Be the Centre', a widely appreciated Vineyard song, is certainly inspired by the Holy Spirit in the way it puts the spotlight on Jesus Christ, God the Son. The words of this song can be found online.[70]

This is in perfect harmony with Jesus' own teaching, as recorded in John's gospel:

14:26: 'The Advocate, the Holy Spirit, whom the Father will send in my name, will teach you all things and will **remind you of everything I have said to you**.'

15:26: 'The Advocate . . . will **testify about me**.'

16:14-15: '**He will glorify me** because it is from me that he will receive what he will make known to you. All that belongs to the Father is mine. That is why I said **the Spirit will receive from me what he will make known to you**.'

---

70. Michael Frye (1999), 'Jesus, be the centre', https://hymnary.org/text/jesus_be_the_centre, (accessed 3.4.24).

The Spirit draws the attention of believers and unbelievers to Jesus, Jesus the Saviour, Lord, Healer, Baptiser, Coming King, the Alpha and Omega. Jesus is central to the Father's redemption plan for humanity, its implementation and consummation, and it is the role of the Holy Spirit to broadcast this to all, be they near or far from the kingdom. The Holy Spirit is wonderfully active in the implementation of the eternal designs that the Father is accomplishing through his beloved Son. Jesus taught that the Spirit's role is to testify to people everywhere of his centrality in the Godhead's eternal purpose.

Dear reader, it could be that the following are part of your past and present experience, or you may have a deep longing for them to become real in your life:

- A clear understanding of the man Jesus, his person, greatness, qualities, teaching, deeds, authority, majesty, his relationship with God the Father and his manner of communicating with children, women and men.

- A grasp of the meaning for humanity of Jesus' death, resurrection and ascension.

- A conviction regarding the grave spiritual and moral condition which is the common heritage of everyone, i.e. we are all sinners and consequently under condemnation and in dire need of a Saviour.

- A heart-warming and relieving assurance that if we confess our sins to God, repent of them and open our lives to Christ, he does come to us to become our personal Saviour, and credit to us his righteousness plus life abundant and eternal.

- A daily walk with the Lord Jesus, living in the light he shines upon us.

You will have noticed that Jesus is central to all of these pilgrimage steps, and to others you may have wanted us to mention! Furthermore, Jesus has told us that it is the Holy Spirit, fulfilling his role, who leads us on from step to step on the pilgrim way. For example, in John 16:7-15 Jesus tells us that it is the Spirit who convicts of sin, righteousness and judgment and points to himself as the only remedy for mankind's desperate moral and spiritual plight.

Jesus, the Christ, is the central theme of the old covenant prophets, the last of whom was John the Baptist who, inspired by the Holy Spirit, boldly announced to his hearers that Jesus was both the propitiatory Lamb of God who takes away the sin of the world, and the one who would baptise disciples with the Holy Spirit.

As a newborn baby Jesus was the centre of attraction, admiration and adoration for a group of Judean shepherds, a smaller group of oriental Magi and his mother and her husband; the Holy Spirit, though the texts make no mention of him, was surely blessedly present in the place where the infant lay. We note that the Magi and Joseph had dreams that guided their actions; dreams are one of the means by which the Holy Spirit leads God's people, and also people to God. It is not uncommon for the Holy Spirit to reveal the person and deity of Jesus to people from a very wide range of backgrounds, including Islam.

When he was 12 Jesus visited Jerusalem with his parents to participate in the Feast of Passover; when it was over he stayed on and soon became the central participant in discussions with the rabbis. The Holy Spirit was with the boy for 'Everyone who heard him was amazed at his understanding and his answers' (Luke 2:47). We would all like to know whether on subsequent visits, as a youth and a young adult, Jesus had further exchanges with the same or perhaps other learned teachers.

Jesus' period of public life, beginning with his baptism in the river Jordan and culminating with his passion, resurrection and ascension, was constantly marked by the presence and actions of the Holy Spirit who unfailingly showed to all who had eyes to see that Jesus is Lord; that he is central and Lord of all, was the Spirit's message to dignitaries, to the common people in field, village and town, to the rich and the poor, to Jews and non-Jews, to the comfortable and the suffering, to crowds and individuals.

It was in the form of a dove that the Holy Spirit descended to alight upon Jesus when he arose from the waters of baptism. Not long afterwards Jesus publicly affirmed that this coming upon him of the Spirit was an anointing that confirmed him to be the Messiah, the Anointed One. Jesus was thereby shown to be unique and the chosen of the Father; he was destined to be the central figure wherever he would go during the remainder of his time on earth, and to an ever-increasing degree thereafter. Jesus made his affirmation during a visit to the synagogue at Nazareth, basing his statement on Isaiah 61:1-2 he said, 'The Spirit of the Sovereign LORD is on me, because the LORD has anointed me to proclaim good news to the poor. He has sent me to bind up the broken-hearted, to proclaim freedom for the captives and release from darkness for the prisoners, to proclaim the year of the LORD's favour' (see Luke 4:18-19).

In the context of our thoughts on the centrality of Jesus we can say that consequent to the Holy Spirit anointing he had received, and which remained on him, Jesus was now centre stage. From then on all eyes would be on him. Many of the onlookers, knowing their need, would believe on him; these would receive riches that the world cannot offer, healing that no doctor was accomplished to effect, deliverance from evil spirits and ruinous lifestyles and liberty from various forms of oppression. There would, however, be other eyes that would see Jesus as an imposter, a blasphemer, a person to despise, to disbelieve and in some cases to hate; for this group of persons Jesus was to become the centre of their preoccupation, the man to be got rid of.

Thumbing through the pages of the four gospels it is plain to see that at event after event, in situation after situation, the key and central figure was always Jesus, and, whether or not he is specifically mentioned, the Holy Spirit was ever there, anointing, enduing, leading on, inspiring the words Messiah used, or the silence he maintained.

- Just prior to visiting the synagogue at Nazareth Jesus 'was led by the Spirit in the wilderness, where for forty days he was tempted by the devil' (Luke 4:1-2). Jesus came through the ordeal victorious and 'returned to Galilee in the power of the Spirit' (4:14).
- In the many encounters he had with individuals (Nicodemus, a Samaritan lady, demon possessed persons).
- Visiting households (Martha, Mary and Lazarus, tax collectors).

- Being with his disciples (on and beside the lake, at the last evening meal they were to share).

- Amongst and in front of crowds (on a hillside and a plain, in Galilee and Jerusalem) and civic and religious authorities (Roman, Jewish).

- When the powers of nature were manifested (storm on Lake Galilee).

- When battling with the powers of darkness (in the Garden, on the cross).

The Acts of the Holy Spirit

As the story in the Book of Acts unfolds it is plain to see that the central figure in the early church was Jesus, the Messiah. Throughout, it is the Holy Spirit's role and pleasure to highlight the Lordship of Jesus, the Christ, to hail him and set him forth as the pre-eminent one at the heart and centre of the Godhead's programme of restoration for humanity and all creation. Ever since those early days the Holy Spirit has continued to fulfil his role, and he does so today within the framework of every local Christian assembly as well as in the Church Universal.

The Church Universal

The Church Universal, the body and bride of Christ, is being formed and perfected in time here on earth and will continue throughout eternity. If we liken her to a wheel, which is constantly getting larger and larger, the rim comprises the vast multitude of the redeemed, those who confess Jesus as Lord and Saviour, the hub or centre, is Jesus, he who holds all things together, and the spokes represent the Holy Spirit who radiates to the rim (the Church Universal) all the attributes of stability, strength, certainty and purpose of the hub. Jesus is the head of his church, his body; he is at the centre; it is via the person and work of the Holy Spirit that all the goodness and holiness in Jesus flows out to his body, his bride.

The centre of a circle or sphere is the point that is equidistant from all points on its circumference. Using this in the context of our illustration, the Church Universal's members are all at an equal distance from their Lord at the centre, and all are beneficiaries, on equal terms, of his attributes which are transmitted to them by the power and efficacy of the Holy Spirit.

Ephesians 1:22-23: 'God placed all things under his [Christ's] feet and appointed him to be head over everything for the church, which is his body, the fullness of him who fills everything in every way.'

Ephesians 5:23: 'Christ is the head of the church, his body, of which he is the Saviour.'

The local community

We can liken the multitude of local churches, assemblies and communities to a very long arrangement of arches, each of which comprises a number of stones, but just a single keystone. In the local community, the arch, all of the components are 'living stones' (1 Peter 2:5) and important, but none so as the keystone, Jesus.

The stone at the top or centre of an arch, dome or vault is known as the keystone, which ensures the viability, stability and strength of the arch under pressure.

Each local 'arch' should function in union and interdependence with the other 'arches' in the same locality, and indeed with 'arches' further afield, with whom the only means of cooperation is by prayer.

The Holy Spirit's ministry is to bind together all of each arch's components, and he does that by working on each 'living stone' to make it compatible with its neighbours, and then by joining the several parts together as a solid, effective whole which draws everyone's attention to the central and all-important keystone, Jesus. Arches joined up make bridges which can connect to peoples and places hitherto unreached by the good news of salvation in Jesus.

The imagery of 1 Peter 2:4-10 is a little different, but readers would certainly find it's teaching complementary to what we have attempted to express.

Revival

Christians caught up in the revival that began in the 1930s in Uganda and spread to other East African countries, and to yet other countries further afield, made a simple but life-transforming discovery. From initially being convinced that the most important element in revival is to experience the inward breaking of being crucified with Christ were led on by the Holy Spirit to realise that, essential as a humbling and breaking experience is, believers must move on to acknowledge and live out the centrality of Jesus. For them revival is not a direct consequence of their being broken and crucified with Christ, but of Christians allowing Jesus to be truly central in their lives.

John 19:18 tells us that Jesus was crucified 'and with him two others – one on each side and Jesus in the middle'. He was on the central cross. Was the Holy Spirit present, drawing attention to the Son of God and his centrality? Not all of the time it would seem, for there was a period when the Son was forsaken by the Father and, we must assume, the Spirit. But once the atoning sacrifice had been made the unity of the Godhead was re-established, and the Father, the Son's own blood and the Spirit together raised up Jesus from the dead. To this, and also to Jesus' ascension, the Holy Spirit bears constant witness (Hebrews 9:14; 10:11-17).

Jesus is our centre of gravity. People are drawn or pulled towards him by the beauty and power of his own person and his works, but also by the attestations and power of the Holy Spirit.

17

The Exhortation of the Spirit in Harmony with Jesus to HEAR

*Whoever has ears, let them hear what
the Spirit says to the churches.*
(Revelation 2:7)

In chapters 2 and 3 of the Book of Revelation we find an exhortation that the ascended Jesus was to send separately to seven churches in seven cities of Asia Minor: Ephesus, Smyrna, Pergamum, Thyatira, Sardis, Philadelphia and Laodicea. The seven Christian communities were each sent a letter containing both commendations and condemnations as appropriate. Each message is concluded with an exhortation to the recipients to 'hear' (see Revelation 2:7,11,17,29; 3:6,13,22), so each community is reminded by Jesus and the Holy Spirit (the Spirit of Jesus) that they have ears to hear, and so they must 'hear what the Spirit says to the churches'.

Similarly, Jesus and his Spirit exhort each of us to hear what the Spirit says to us in these days.

Bibliography

Adam Clarke, *Commentary on Galatians* (CreateSpace Independent Publishing Platform, 2015), Kindle Edition.

Adam Clarke, *Commentary on Matthew* (Pokeno, NZ: Titus Books, 2013), Kindle Edition.

Alexander Cruden, *Cruden's Complete Concordance to the Bible* (Cambridge: The Lutterworth Press, 1977).

Brother Lawrence, *The Practice of the Presence of God* (London: Hodder & Stoughton, 1981).

C.S. Lewis, *Mere Christianity* (New York: Touchstone, a division of Simon & Schuster, 1996).

Harold Horton, *The Gifts of the Spirit* (Springfield, MO: Gospel Publishing House, 1975).

Harold Morton, *Messages that Made the Revival* (London: Epworth Press, 1920).

Howard A. Snyder, *Signs of the Spirit: How God Reshapes the Church* (Eugene, OR: Wipf & Stock Publishers, 1997).

Jamieson, Fausset and Brown, *Commentary Practical and Explanatory on the Whole Bible* (London: Oliphants Ltd, 1961).

Matthew Henry's Commentary on the Whole Bible, Complete and Unabridged in One Volume (Peabody MA: Hendrickson Publishers, 1991).

NIV Study Bible (London: Hodder & Stoughton, 1987).

Redemption Hymnal (London: Assemblies of God Publishing House, 1955).

Roy Hession, *The Calvary Road* (Buckingham, UK: Rickfords Hill Publishing, 2010).

George Stormont, *Smith Wigglesworth, A Man Who Walked with God* (Tulsa, OK: Harrison House, 1989).

Wesley's Standard Sermons, Volume I (London: Epworth Press, 1951).

Wesley's Standard Sermons, Volume II (London: Epworth Press, 1951).